Breakout

by Ralph Moore

illustrated by
John Gretzer

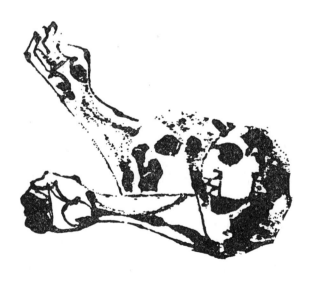

FRIENDSHIP PRESS   NEW YORK

All Bible quotations used in this book are from the Revised
Standard Version, copyright, 1946 and 1952, by the Division
of Christian Education of the National Council of the Churches
of Christ in the United States of America.

Library of Congress Catalog Card Number: 68-14058
Copyright © 1968 by FRIENDSHIP PRESS, INC.
Printed in the United States of America.

CONTENTS

1 Bags

A group of youth and adults were meeting for the weekend to discuss youth's role in the church. The church building in which they met was a fabulous piece of architecture, designed by one of the world's greatest architects just before he died. The people now gathered were seventy or so typical, ordinary middle-class Protestant high school students, adult leaders and clergymen, black and white.

Such was the scene on that Saturday afternoon in February. A denominational youth secretary, the visiting "expert," was charged with the job of putting something sensible, meaningful, relevant, challenging and inspiring into those eager, devoted, hungry, captive minds and hearts.

The Friday night and Saturday morning sessions had come off well. He had shown good films—that will always grab a group. Mid-twentieth-century people most easily and quickly communicate through electronic circuitry: telephone, radio, records, television, electric guitar, microphone and film.

But now a human voice had to feed words into the process, and the speaker was overcome by the fear that had been plaguing him more often as he advanced in age: the fear that most words fail utterly to say anything real in the midst of a culture absorbed in sound, color, motion and instantaneous data processing. Words are not as crucial as they used to be. They are slow and require time to be understood in an era of "now" people.

On that particular Saturday afternoon everybody sat around in a close circle as the speaker had a kind of dialogue with another man about new forms of work in which youth and adults are trying to do some new things about certain social issues of concern to Christians. It was a descriptive rundown of significant breakthroughs in several towns and cities. Then the discussion opened up for total group free-for-all.

People began to pounce on the speaker with questions: "Well, what is the purpose of the church, anyway?" and "How do we know what God's will is?" and other supertopics, which the truly huge minds of history have yet to handle adequately.

Before long the youth themselves were engaged in hot debate. Most of them made strong statements, such as:

"The church's mission is to proclaim the gospel so that more people can lead lives that please God."

"The church's mission is to teach people proper moral values and ideals."

"The church's mission is to convert people to a belief in Christianity."

The speaker kept his mouth shut, but he was a little bewildered by his impression that these contemporary young people actually believed the platitudes and clichés they were tossing off so easily.

Then came the corker: "The church's mission is to lead people to Christ so that they can go to heaven." For the next half hour the group devoted itself to the proposition that God is really loving and does not keep an African native out of heaven just because he has not been exposed to Christianity—and the same is true even for some Communists. It was apparent that most of us saw the church as having a certain possession, which mankind needs if it is to be saved from hell.

"The church's mission is to baptize all men in the name of Jesus Christ and make them his disciples. That's what the Bible says, doesn't it?"

"If everyone in the world was a Christian then we wouldn't have all the wars and conflicts we have now, would we, and there would be more brotherhood and love."

At that point the "guest speaker" had to break in. "This whole conversation is irrelevant! What is all this heaven-hell talk? I disagree with just about everything I've heard this afternoon. Man, this is the twentieth century! There's an unbelievable mess out there in the big world! What does all our talk really mean to it? Or even to us, for that matter?"

There was a hushed and hostile silence. Eyes seemed to penetrate straight through him as he resumed. He was terribly aware that he had taken a rather arrogant, over-simplified approach and that with the next few words he could easily muff it. "I really get ticked off when a bunch of swinging cats like you swallow a lot of old ideas and call it religion. You know what The Mamas and The Papas say about that kind of stuff, 'You oughta know by now, words of love, soft and tender, won't win a girl's heart anymore; worn-out phrases and longing gazes won't get you where you want to go,' and if that's the way it is with love, baby, what's with all this talk that'll convince the whole world?" [1]

After the group's laughter died away, he continued. "Your idea of converting people to Christianity has got to go. That's not our job, really. That's not the real mission of the church at this moment in history. We're not in the business of turning everybody into Christians."

There was much reaction and anger in the group.

"Look, here's my idea of mission," the leader went on. "We—the church—have the task of *doing* things, not just *saying* things. The gospel—what's that? It's new breaks for people whose lives are all rotten breaks, bad news.

"Our job is to get with this moment in history and try to understand what might be good news in situations where all hell is breaking loose, quite literally. It's a fantastically big and complex world. There are no simple sayings. Political hang-ups and social customs and traditional values keep all kinds of injustices going. We're supposed to knock down barriers and build up humans.

"Actually, gospel really means becoming more human over against the pressures that tend to dehumanize us, such as pressures to get into college, pressures to keep the

[1] Notes may be found on p. 128.

rats from biting your children, pressures to keep you in your place because you're black, and so on. These pressures dehumanize because they put people out of shape, instead of enhancing their capacities to be full persons. It's a fabulous, exciting, groovy—and hideous—thing to be a live human being, and be a Christian, because it means that you've got to wire into everything, seriously, and get plugged into all the stuff that makes the world what it is. This Christian scene is really life-long. Your guts are included, see, not just the brains, and . . . well, end of sermon!"

The chaotic clamor that followed this oratory resembled the final moments of a thirty-lap stock car race: vehicles clashing and spinning in every direction, wreckage, smoke, shouting and beautiful urgency, drama.

Maybe the blast was a bit overdone. But it released some passion, and it did steer the group away from the dead ends it had been facing as long as it used the old slogans of the church. What seemed important at the moment was the need for everyone to explore more of who they themselves thought they were, their own feelings and perceptions of the real world, and then discuss Christianity in terms of the present age as they understood it.

All of us live in bags, very much like the plastic sandwich bags available in any supermarket. We see everything through the sides of the bags we inhabit. The bags are all preconceived notions: bags of racial identity, class, background, school values, national pride, age group, religion, personal fears and countless other prejudices. The Catholic who hates the Protestant looks out through the sides of his own Catholic bag. The same goes for the Protestant who hates the Catholic, and all the non-Jews see the Jew strictly through their non-Jewish bags. We learn from early age to function according to these bags; our parents and our friends help fashion the bags we live in.

The first job of one who desires to be really human is to undertake a study of the bags in which one lives. We've got to become aware of them from the start. Jesus and Paul, Moses, Isaiah, Jeremiah, Amos and all of the great figures then and since then have really been anxious to make people aware of their bags, and then to help them poke holes in their bags, let in new vision of what is outside, and then help people completely rip open the sides of the bags and climb out. We climb into other bags as we leave the old ones, to be sure, but the new bags are, we hope, bigger bags with wider views of what the real world is like. Perhaps all of life for alive people is spent in the process of poking holes in all the bags in which they find themselves, so that new air, new involvement, new perception of life can happen, bringing to each a sense of new humanity. What we must seek to do when we are together is to help each other open each other's eyes a little wider and see more of life's possibilities and urgencies.

At this point I had best confess openly that I was the "guest speaker" in the fiasco mentioned at the beginning of this chapter. I hope that in those hours we did poke some holes in some bags.

I was next involved for a few days in a large city, less than two hours away in flight time. As the airliner took off, part of my heated brain was already exploring the streets and looking into people's faces there. Then my thoughts jumped to my wife and son, three thousand miles away in Philadelphia. Then to a friend in Prague, Czechoslovakia, on to hungry masses in India, to the struggling leaders of African society, to a student I know in Argentina, to the

Red Guards on Chinese streets, and finally to the savage spectacle of Vietnam, where millions are forced to live out the absurdities of modern warfare and political bloodshed.

"It's out of one bag and into another," I almost said out loud to the stewardess. Will we ever get to where we see things in one total human bag that encompasses the whole earth? Even as the earth-bag is being probed by NASA, humans haven't learned that they belong to a single family.

As though looking for an answer to my own question, I flipped open a book of poetry and saw this one by Richard Brautigan:

PSALM

A farmer
in Eastern
Oregon saw
Jesus in
a chicken
house.
Jesus was
standing
there,
holding
a basket
of eggs.
Jesus said,
"I'm hungry."
The farmer
never
told what
he saw
to anyone.[2]

2 Urban-Suburban

Anthony Quinn, dressed up like an Eskimo, was grunting around on the peeling paint and cracking plaster. The dogs barked as he yelled "Mush!" at them, and the white missionary was always frightened and repulsed by Anthony Quinn and all the other crude people whom he had been sent to save. Every time the blue sky or the white snow would come into focus during the arguments and the fights, the sagging, dirty wall reminded you where you were.

Thirty or forty youth, some very young and some older, were crammed into the Quiet Place, a center in an old store on the south side section of Chicago called Kenwood. At

14

least one night a week they watch a feature film projected on the end wall of the Quiet Place. Sponsored by a local Mennonite congregation, the Quiet Place really belongs to the neighborhood. There is not much organization to it. It just is. Several adults and youth, black and white, more or less keep track of what's going on and what help is needed. But overall, the youth themselves call the shots.

Anthony Quinn, dressed up like an Eskimo, refused to believe and act the way the white missionary wanted him to. For example, when he explained that he cheerfully loaned out his wife to other men from time to time, the missionary scolded him and gave him a lecture on Christian morals. Anthony Quinn just laughed at him. So did the kids in the Quiet Place. Most of them were black and they could immediately identify with the Eskimo's defiance against the white missionary. Finally, Eskimo Quinn said, "Don't come to me with your laws. I have no use for them. I live by my own. White man from different world. Go back home." The kids in the Quiet Place cheered.

When the film ended anyone could grab a hot dog, something to drink, do any of a number of things, or leave. More than half of the youth there that night sat around talking about the Anthony Quinn Eskimo film. I had never seen it before, and thought it was corny melodrama. I was obviously not responding from where the kids were. To them it was a perfect statement of the dilemma in which they, in the inner city of Chicago, felt very caught and captive. In a real way the white missionary had represented all white men authority figures, with power to make and enforce the laws, run the schools, collect the rent for your slum apartment, hire and fire you at will, run the stores and send you to Vietnam to fight for freedom and democracy. The Quiet Place was hardly quiet that night, and as

15

I walked out onto the street I felt a shudder that had nothing to do with the chilly air. I had just experienced a complete shredding of one of my bags. These kids had ventilating to do. Their experiences with whites had been too intense and unjust for them to quickly or easily trust me, who had walked in there that night in the image of white-man missionary, ready to do good and provide things for the unfortunate, underprivileged people.

My host was the Rev. Ray Gillies. He and his wife had lived in Kenwood for several years, and although he was formally related to the Kenwood United Church of Christ, his primary image in the neighborhood was that of a detached guy, beholden to nobody, and free to mix it up with anyone whenever a situation arose. The long history of suspicion that inner city people usually bring to relationships with clergy and lay members of big churches had been broken where Ray and his wife, Jay were concerned. They were trusted, a fantastic thing to be able to say about any white guy living in Kenwood.

"Our ideas of morality," Ray said, "our ideas of law, our ideas of what the good life is—these kids aren't ready to buy any of it, and I don't think they ever will. The churches have got to understand that our little moral judgments—like sexual behavior—are secondary. The real mission is in terms of a larger morality, the morality of the way Cook County politics gums up the War on Poverty, the way incompetent teachers manhandle the kids at school, the problems faced by the kids who drop out, the snooty, white middle-class values brought in by social workers who call these people 'clients,' as though they were sick or something. We've got to recognize that people who live in Kenwood are terrific human beings with lots of potential. We've got to encourage them to use it—on *their* terms."

16

Ray Gillies spends all his time taking people seriously on their own terms. His is a ministry of listening, of waiting, of being present and of caring what happens to people even when they turn their backs on him. He brings to each moment a readiness to laugh and a spirit of swinging loose. He is also a hardheaded politician. For Ray, mission takes place in the middle of the tough battle of confounding the schemes of political and economic planners who don't understand what they are doing to people who aren't like them. "They usually assume," Ray says, "that everybody ought to want to be white and middle class and live in suburbs. We've got to take the message to them that this just ain't so."

Ray's approach is that the kids themselves, in their own natural groups, including gangs, should be encouraged to develop their own style of community activity, whether that be sports or some back-to-school tutoring process.

A few nights later Ray and I dropped into the Quiet Place again. Half the young people there were white. They had come into Kenwood from Chicago suburbs like Hinsdale, Longview and Des Plaines, all rather nice, white communities. They belonged to churches in those cities. They came down to Kenwood or some Kenwood kids went out to them at least once a month, sometimes more frequently. They all identified with each other. It was the Urban-Suburban group, commonly called US.

US came about because of a summer conference experience in which Ray and several other leaders decided to risk an intercultural camp in which black youth from the center of Chicago and white youth from suburban churches would spend at least a week together. Almost a disaster because of the great differences, this event (called Project REACH) resulted in human beings discovering each other through

17

their many bags of suspicion and ill will. When the week came to a close, they insisted that the group not split up. That is when the US group came into existence.

I felt the same way when out in Oak Lawn, a suburb south and west of Chicago, the US group met and scared everyone for miles around. Who was this group of blacks swarming into their community? What kind of parents would let their kids associate with "them"? I am sure that it was no coincidence that the police arrived to guarantee our silence as we made our way from the church building to cars to go for a pizza after the program had concluded.

The US group operates on the fundamental hunch that all human beings have the capacity for being human. Some people, oddly enough, will not buy a statement like that. Ray Gillies and his bunch of fellow workers all do, and you can see it work in the US group. We will never rub out racial and economic differences in personal relationships, no matter how close. But we can appreciate one another's humanity and learn how to enjoy our differences. As a result, there is a kind of celebration always in the air, as though everyone were about to sing. From time to time they do hold celebrations, a form of worship where freedom songs and their own readings and discussions revolve around a meal together.

Then there is the HUB, a dynamism composed largely of kids who live in Kenwood—black, impatient, desirous of doing something in the political-social arena of conflict and of getting results. Through arrangements with the YMCA, HUB is opening the way for some youth who dropped out of school to get some further education.

HUB has also put together and taken to the suburbs an excellent production of *In White America*, a scathing commentary on the dominant culture from the standpoint of black Americans. This is a powerful form of communication; their own initiative has built the production, and the work of HUB has provided new openings for each participant to see more possibilities for himself.

As I sat in the Quiet Place among the US group I wondered how long this thing would keep going. At the moment they were strongly animated. The atmosphere was totally joyous—but also incredibly profound.

"We've got to let all you white cats out there in the upper middle class ghettos sweat a little and worry some about what's gonna happen. Then we gonna come out there and save you from yourself, man."

Everyone cheered and coaxed the boy who was speaking at the moment. "I mean, like, Mayor Daley can't stop us and Martin Luther King can't start us. We got to do it ourselves. We're livin' in one city, one whole place, one metropolis, as them city hall cats like to say it. Me-trop-oh-lissss. That's it. Don't stop at Chicago city limits. You in it too, baby."

A tall white boy, turtleneck sweater, interrupted. "You're right. I know that. We know that. Lots of people know that. *But,* how do we get the message through to people like our parents, eh? I mean, look at our churches out there. They just automatically underwrite everything the adults, our parents, you know, anything they want. I mean, that's why we moved out there—to get away from the dregs of humanity like you." He pointed his finger at the other boy and looking around asked, "Right?" Everyone roared in Bill Cosby fashion, "Right!"

"Baby, you got to carry on a revolution out there, man. That's the church's real thing. That's the only thing Jesus woulda wanted—revolution, pure and simple. I mean, you may say to yourselves, 'Well, we're only young people and

19

therefore cannot do a single thing.' I tell you, you got your head someplace else if that's what you think."

It suddenly occurred to me how unlike the other night this moment was. In the one instance Anthony Quinn, dressed up like an Eskimo, had been resisting the mistaken claims and instructions of the zealous white missionary who intended to save him and the other unredeemed people of his village. The all-black youth audience had reacted with beautiful honesty, for that had been a film of stereotypes that acted out the painful drama of their predicament. Now, in the same room, and with many of the same black youth involved, white and black were relating to each other as human persons. There appeared to be no desire on anyone's part to be like someone else. Somehow they had put their fingers on the key idea of the church's mission in an urban world: black and white, inner city and suburb, lower and middle class, totally different in all respects, grappling for ways to build in the urban area.

The major motif, repeated often, was interdependence. A person in Hinsdale could not consider himself totally human any longer without identifying himself with his brother in Kenwood. And the identification was not paternalistic, condescending, as though Hinsdale had the keys to the kingdom. His identification was born out of a sense of outrage over the injustices of the inner city, which kept his brother down. He felt impatient if he could not work at solving some of those political and economic hang-ups down there. In US, the political and economic hang-ups were continually confronted through meetings at the Quiet Place and the activities of other organizations, such as Operation Breadbasket of the Southern Christian Leadership Conference, a movement to support black manufacturers and businesses. Furthermore, a person from the suburbs began to see the dignity of his black brother, and so looked up to him with respect and admiration. He really needed to know him as a friend.

On the other hand, a young person from Kenwood might help suburbanites recognize some of the unfortunate deprivations they were suffering as a result of their homogeneous isolation. And it was possible that he, himself, might learn something new about white people: that they are not all intent upon exploiting black people, for example. It is also possible that his own perceptions of the greater world and its possibilities for him might expand through his relationships with people in such a strange and faraway land as a suburb.

What is happening at US in Chicago is starting to take place in many urban areas. Churches are developing their ministries on a broader scale, considering the entire metropolitan area to be a single, dynamic reality. Even in Los Angeles now, in what is called the Goals Project, all of the hundreds and hundreds of square miles of city and county areas are considered one organism, totally interdependent. Every large city is now coming of age in this respect, coming to comprehend itself as a single unit of commerce, industry, residential communities, educational institutions, rapid transit, law enforcement, social welfare and finally, political process.

Developments in the Toronto metropolitan area demonstrate this same process. Stewart Crysdale describes similar movements in his little volume, *Churches Where the Action Is!* The interaction among youth and adults who are trying to develop new bases for a ministry that takes seriously the total complex of a Canadian urban community is significant for its ecumenical vigor. People who live in the United States usually overlook, furthermore, the interdependencies of "international" cities, such as Detroit–Windsor.

It seems that youth, those now in high school, are better prepared than anyone ever has been to deal with cities in creative ways. They are more mobile than any other generation has been, and they have been wired into the outside world through the mass media from their birth. Due to technological advance they are practically oriented around the idea that anything man really decides he wants to do can be done. Furthermore, youth today are more suspicious than ever of the clichés and prejudices of a former generation. Their natural desire to rebel and try things for themselves contributes to the possibility that they might learn how to deal with the complex issues of urban life. These ideas were impressed upon me as the evening wore on at the Quiet Place.

Then I pondered how this all had come about. The answer: church commitment. In Kenwood, Hinsdale, Toronto—everywhere, churches abound. There are hundreds of them. But it took the Mennonites to found the Quiet Place, and it took Ray Gillies to pledge himself to what he was doing. And it took the support of other church bodies to keep Ray and his wife housed, fed and clothed. After Ray had begun to open up the channels to suburban churches, others joined him, and a real thing began to build. Everyone brought a different image of the church to the crisis. Everyone had a different expectation of what would happen. After nearly three years, they are beginning to hold a common idea of what the church's mission is, at least for them. Congregations in the suburbs have had to re-evaluate what they thought youth work was supposed to be before they could be willing to see their young people dropping much of the traditional activity and joining US.

My thoughts were interrupted by a blast of words. An argument had erupted between two suburban girls who had always expressed hesitancy when the more revolutionary ideas seemed to be on top.

"But how is all of this any different from any other group? What's the church side of it? Aren't we supposed to have some kind of spiritual job to do?"

"What's more spiritual than working for justice and putting love into action?"

"No. That's not exactly what I mean. I mean aren't we supposed to be teaching something—you know, leading people to Christ, or something?"

Walking away from the Quiet Place I recalled the dozens of places I had had the same debate. Are we not supposed to be changing people into Christians? That's at the center of it. What is mission if it is not winning people to the Christian point of view?

Ernie Southcott, the Anglican rector in Leeds, England, has always insisted that the church neither brings people to Christ nor Christ to people. Rather, the church is supposed to do things that expose Christ, who is already in motion in the world itself.

What are those things? To put it briefly, what the US group is doing actually acts out and brings people into the basic, loving, humanizing intention that Christianity has always called God's will. We know that the approach of the white missionary to Anthony Quinn, dressed up like an Eskimo, was wrong, for he violated the personality of another individual and he brought demands based upon another culture and another religious perspective. We recognize how the church's mission cannot be found in the posture of coercing people into believing in God or even into acting like those of us who think that we are Christians. The US group avoids all of that. It begins with human beings, in all of their less than perfect integrity. And then it opens ways for them to do something about the total human situation.

It all has to do with being human ourselves, and out of our growing understanding of what it means to be human —glory and imperfection—responding to all events in life; personal events and great social, even international, events. We've got to act as those who experience the humanity and inhumanity of the world. Can any of us truly watch the televised Asian war without human feelings? Yes, most people do. The US group, and the others around the world like them, cannot. From Jane Stembridge in Mississippi comes a great word about this:

> *SOMEONE sat and told me*
> *something new*
> *I'm taking off*
> *Out there a mile or more*
> *is*
> *meadows where the soft green*
> *summer children go*
> *I'd like a lot*
> *to look at them*
> *a little while,*
> *remember being small of*
> *curlied hair*
> *and loved*
> *and let alone*
> *to use my fingertips*
> *even on*
> *the grownups pretty hands*

That certainly was
a long time ago
but never mind
my buddy boy
I understand your crucifix
Come on
we'll walk a way
we know already how to
climb a hill
and here's the simple plan:
I lift the wire
while you go underneath.
You lift the wire
for me.[1]

3 The Arts

Several large paintings were stacked against the east wall of the studio. They were about all one could see through the window from the outside. The painter was supposed to be there to meet me for a conversation about his work, but I seemed to be out of luck. I knew that he and his wife were having difficulties, and that his children were of great concern to him now that a divorce or separation appeared inevitable. I didn't blame him for not being around his studio to talk to someone he had never met.

The artist had been known around the Boston area for the fresh, new, penetrating style in his painting. Out here in the middle of the New England woods several miles west of Boston, one could easily withdraw from the entire world and paint fields and flowers. This man had been suffering through the agony of the world's predicaments, however, and had been trying to make some kind of statement in oils and other materials about his perceptions and convictions, particularly about race. I had hoped to invite him personally to be with a group that was organizing a conference on the arts to be held in the summer.

Driving back to Boston, I was told how the artist had become a friend of a couple who were developing a ministry in the arts through their church in a small Massachusetts town. I had seen the most recent exhibit there of paintings, sculptures and constructions, and had been very impressed. "The important thing," the wife had said, "is that we hope to relate to artists in a respectably professional way so that they will be free to be human beings around us church people. This is always the problem. Hanging their work up on the wall is only a small part of it. Giving a platform from which their artistic insights about existence can be confronted is the most important thing we try for."

I asked her if she thought the artist whom we had just tried to meet would come to our summer conference. "I doubt it. Like so many artists, he suspects the church, its motives and its ways of thinking. He'll probably be happy to send some of his canvases, but I doubt that he will want to confront a lot of people he doesn't know well and therefore doesn't trust."

I knew that she was right. And I knew exactly how he felt.

A metal sculptor in Oregon, for example, had told me of his dilemma during the heated period of the freedom movements in the South during 1963. "Sometimes I think I'm immoral for spending all my time out here in my barn in the middle of Oregon fir trees," he said. "I know that people are getting hanged and beaten and burned and tortured in Mississippi. And I know that a lot doesn't get done and that all the students who are joining up with SNCC and CORE and the other groups need my support and even, maybe, my body with them down there—now. Almost every day I get up and wonder all over again just what the hell I'm supposed to be doing with myself. But I end up taking my metal and my blow torch and my hammer and my snips and beating out more copper, or whatever it is at the moment. I've got three or four different pieces going at the same time and I've got to finish them, that's all. It's a necessity for me to complete them. And before I'm done with them, naturally, three or four more are on the way. It's like having babies. But it's all hell for me—and heaven, too—and the only way I can handle it is to finally say to myself that I'm doing an important, responsible thing. I mean, the world needs art. It's got to have it. How else is it going to remember what some of the big human questions of existence are, I mean, except through literature and the visual arts, dramas and films and so forth? In other words, I think of myself out here as doing a responsible human thing. I think all artists, whatever they're doing, are responsible human beings first and artists second."

A few months later Deering, New Hampshire was the scene. Many artists from Canada and the United States—painters, sculptors, actors, directors, writers, poets, dancers, musicians, film makers, critics and composers descended on the church conference center there for what turned out to be a ten-day happening. The purpose was to explore the topic, "The Church, The Arts and Human Creativity." Some of the persons from local churches and church-related educational institutions think to this day that we never discussed the topic. Others, including the artists, came away overwhelmed by how deeply we had gotten into not only the topic, but also ourselves as people.

Sensitive about how artists often view the church's rigidity, we had purposely refused to work out a careful schedule for the ten days. In other words, anyone could get up and eat a continental breakfast of coffee and rolls anytime of the day. And there were very few organized meetings or discussion groups. Most of the time was free for people to work on a print press that a painter from Philadelphia had brought, or read, or discuss things with someone, or swim in the lake. We had some dramatic events under "production" from time to time, and a composer would meet with a group of people occasionally for improvisation on a variety of instruments. And every night parties were held in various cottages or at the main building. Records were being played, dancing and singing burst forth and very penetrating debates erupted. It was like a gigantic house party. No one had to conform to everything that went on.

Before many days had passed a community of persons had begun to take shape, persons who, across their various categories—Christian, Jew, agnostic, clergyman, painter, church school teacher, denominational administrator, actor —discovered new excitement in having their own little bags broken open. And some rather significant insights began to emerge about how the church and the arts ought to be rediscovering each other after so many centuries of mutual suspicion.

Dr. Clemens Benda, a psychiatrist, described how an

artist must, almost by the nature of his artistic act, suffer through alienation from society. The creative person, in his view, is one whose vision of new imperatives for man in the world extends far beyond the present moment into a future that he sees with clarity. In addition to this, the creative person recalls and relives with great intensity the primary experiences of his childhood, those vivid moments of feeling and shock and joy and discovery and pain that have propelled him into the present. The creative person, then, is held in a tension between the freshness of his past and the not yet fulfilled future, and he explores this in what he does at the here and now intersection of his human existence.

Artists are real human beings, one discovers, not desirous of being categorized out of the center of the society, but nonetheless aware that they bring to people difficult material that requires involvement and arouses hostilities.

The Deering scene erupted at big moments, such as the evening when we spontaneously staged a film premiere in honor of Robert Newman, a film maker whose film, 5½, was shown in its final form for the first time. It was a rather psychedelic evening: strange music, wild colored posters, actors soaring highly in their imitations of famous people, and most of the conference-goers arriving in their cars, horns blaring, in "hippie" costume.

After several days of this kind of thing, one of the disgusted onlookers said of us, "They're acting like a bunch of adolescents." And that very remark provided the key to the whole affair. Though offered as a negative judgment, it was precisely right in the most positive sense. Here were adults—artists and church people—discovering once again together, in their mutual experiences, some of the spontaneity, the rebellion, the freshness and the pain of what it is to be an alive human being, growing up, confronting one's whole self and celebrating life's possibilities. This became the premise on which all of our reflections afterward were based. The artists' bags had been broken in new ways and so had the others'.

The Religion and Theatre Council of Canada exercises leadership in the arts. It helps bring actors, playwrights and production-minded people of parishes into communication with one another. It has even helped the commissioning of new plays. Hilda Powicke, a fine writer, has written several good one-act plays for use in churches, a most notable one being *Coffeehouse,* a simple, straightforward situation drama about acceptance and forgiveness in a complex city. The Council tries to keep track of churches that attempt new things and then encourages people of the community in general to support them in every possible way.

The magnificence of Expo 67 in Montreal lay in its new artistic discoveries, not only in drama but in film, mixed media and architecture. The "Christian" exhibitions were done with great taste and commitment to excellence. Many of the pavilions, such as the Czechoslovakian, created new dialogue between man in his social predicament and the work of artists. In fact, many critics have hailed the entire event of Expo 67 as a major artistic accomplishment. Such groups as the National Film Board of Canada were influential in communicating through this international spectacle the importance of imagination for economic and political planners.

The arts have the capacity to move people into renewed social consciousness, and they are finding new places and unexpected settings. The Inglewood Community Players in Inglewood, Nova Scotia, began producing a new play during the summer of 1967 entitled, "Coming Here to Stay," written by a young poet, David Giffin, a recent graduate of Dalhousie University. The play dramatizes a surprising feature of Canadian history: the difficult struggle for human dignity of the black people who live in Nova Scotia. About 14,000 Negroes live there, forty percent of the Negro population of the entire nation of Canada. Most of them flocked there from the Southern slave states during the War of 1812. Not many of us would have become aware of the destitution of spirit and the continual invisibility of these people had not the Nova Scotia Centennial Committee on the Arts produced this play, which has toured parts of Quebec and Ontario since its initial runs in the Halifax area. In fact, how many of us could have imagined the existence of the Nova Scotia Association for the Advancement of Colored People before this artistic event?

Sometimes the artist clarifies for us who we are or want to be. Let us consider some examples.

The world never looks the same after one has let the artistic vision poke holes through the bags one inhabits. That is why it is unfortunate when people try to turn off the arts, such as the congregation in Florida that fired its pastor and cited, among other things, that he took the church's youth to see the film, *A Patch of Blue*.

Samuel Beckett's play, *Endgame*, brings the audience to the edge of despair. Two strange, decadent characters, on a stage of drab grays and blacks, rattle on for more than an hour in charged dialogue that deals with their misery about being alive. They have figured out how to wait for the end —by playing endless games of cruelly contrived tricks on each other. It all amounts to the "end-game," which, the playwright asserts, may be all anybody can do throughout life; that is, to endure an absurd existence while waiting for the final defeat, the conclusion of a meaningless trek through human experience. And so we must endure these gruesome characters in their painful boredom that quickly overtakes us and makes us squirm for fresh air even while we are being entertained.

After a recent production of this play the director told some of us that a psychiatrist had brought one of his patients to see the play. She was a sixteen-year-old girl who had tried to commit suicide three times. Why this play, we asked the doctor. Why such a hopeless statement as this for a girl already wallowing in fear and depression? The psychiatrist pointed out that, on the contrary, this play opened up entirely new channels of hope for the girl. At last, in her experience, she had been confronted by an event enacted by other living persons—writer and actors—who totally identified with her. They knew how she felt. This was worth months of therapy for her. The communion with a few other real people in life had been an opening up of joy for her. She had virtually danced out of the theater that night.

What is important, above all, is that the arts be taken seriously in and of themselves, and that the artist's work, his perception, be allowed to live freely in our midst, without our placing theological frameworks around it, superimposing our ready-made clichés about God onto it, or simply treating it as an "in" thing to do, that is, having contemporary art decorating our walls, even though we have no intention of dealing with it.

On a snowy evening a small group of youth and adults gathered in a church social hall in New London, Wisconsin, a small farming community. We were supposed to discuss, in a few words or less, the tiny topic of "The New Morality." We could not have been in a more unlikely place or frame of mind to tackle such a scorcher. We thought that we could break it open, however, by the combined effect and extreme intensity of several art forms all at once. About thirty people sat around on the floor, therefore, tearing out of magazines and newspapers any items that grabbed them strongly—editorials, cartoons, news stories, advertisements. They were told to keep them in their hands ready for instantaneous use.

Then it began. First, on the movie screen at one end of the room appeared a film, *The Squeeze*, a poignant art film about the population explosion. Moments later a television set flashed on "The Man from U.N.C.L.E." Soon, Phil Ochs could be heard from the other end of the room, and then the voice of a local radio newscaster. A music student began to play on a piano and clarinet alternately, and a tape recorder suddenly echoed with the sounds of a traditional Sunday morning worship service. Meanwhile, back on the floor, persons began to read out loud the clippings they had chosen—louder and louder as more of them joined in. And finally, someone started flipping the room lights off and on, creating grotesque patterns of shadows, darkness and then blinding light.

Chaos, pandemonium, wild screaming and an increasing activity quickly built up in the room. People began wadding up their newspapers and throwing them at each other. Some people stood up, walked around and beat on chairs. A guitar player circulated through the jumping crowd. Suddenly, totally unexpectedly, a man stood on a chair and cursed the group into silence. The electronic instruments stopped. "I've got to rage. This does it! Listen!" He said, "It says here that the only viable alternative to our present policy in Vietnam is to pursue a totally military victory at the earliest possible moment. This will require that we intensify our bombing of North Vietnam, escalate our ground action and press for the total destruction of the enemy at all costs." Said the reader: "This guy really bugs me." Jumping to his feet, a student shouted, "You son-of-a-bitch!"

Here was confrontation with the highest moral problems confronting the human race. Here was ventilation and intensification and confrontation. The group had begun to do its work and to come to terms with the real world of conflicting claims in a realistic, honest atmosphere of free inquiry into the issues. The following hours were productive for us all; we had gotten into the guts of our feelings as well as into the important material itself. And a great host of artists had been with us, through their works, to push us to this brink.

The snow was still falling as I flew out of Wisconsin a short time later. The Beatles were on television that week singing *Strawberry Fields.* It was all a collage of gauze and wire and pinpoints. And it symbolized for me one of the frontiers of the church's mission—the creative edges of the arts. By this I mean both the arts in their most familiar forms, and the arts as they are being newly explored, in the multi-media experiments, happenings, light shows and totally open-ended bombardments of films, slides, music and live action.

The coffeehouse atmospheres, which engender and support these experiments, are becoming commonplace. But coffeehouses are not the cure-alls of an ailing church. They do, upon occasion, when they are conceived in a very informal, genuine setting, provide the environment that communicates new possibilities for human beings. The coffeehouse has always been a place where social protest has been freely expressed. The rise of "angry" artists has not been merely a twentieth century phenomenon, but in our day we have witnessed new bursts of energy in people of all ages and backgrounds who suddenly come alive to guitars, singing, writing, acting or organizing ways for the artistic expressions of others to be confronted.

The stewardess brought me a copy of *Life* Magazine. Its feature article dealt with happenings. You can't get away from art any more. This is a new day for the church to comprehend the culture and move with the arts into the big issues, for reviving the ancient unity of artists and Christian mission, when artists from within designed the buildings and the vessels and the festivals, the music and the drama, that together formed the worship service itself. We are on the threshold of truly basic endeavors. Excellent composers and fine poets are writing new hymns of celebration reflecting what late twentieth century man is like. We are totally reshaping the styles of worship, reconceiving what our services are supposed to be doing.

Shoving aside the copy of *Life*, I picked up my newspaper. On the front page was a report of the controversy between Pope Paul and those Roman Catholic leaders in Europe who are experimenting with jazz, folk and rock music in the mass. It's everywhere. The doors have been flung open. No longer can the arts be treated as nice things to have around; they are becoming understood as essential to the very existence of Christianity. With a sigh of exhilaration I stared out into the black of night, catching a glimpse of the moon through the mist.

Somehow, this all adds up. This all takes us somewhere closer to the real world in which human beings live. And of such is the church's mission in a new day. And some lines from a favorite poem by Stanley Kunitz jumped to my mind:

Let me proclaim it—human be my lot!—
How from my pit of green horse-bones
I turn, in a wilderness of sweat,
To the moon-breasted sibylline,
And lift this garland, Danger, from her throat
To blaze it in the foundries of the night.[1]

4 Protest

My knuckles were freezing white and my teeth chattering. I had failed to wear a warm coat and it was eight o'clock in the morning. Even though the sun was shining, West 123rd Street on Manhattan Island sported a moist, chilling breeze that went right through me.

But I was warming up inside as I spoke to some of the people who carried picket signs in front of P.S. 125, a New York City elementary school. One was a Puerto Rican mother from Harlem. Another was the wife of a professor at Columbia University. Another was a black laborer. The group was composed of ten or eleven persons of very different backgrounds who had discovered something in common—they had children attending the same school. They were part of a larger movement that had been meeting for several months to express a concern for the quality of the education their children were receiving. Failing to receive any satisfying hearing from school administrators, they were now staging a boycott of the school itself. Of the 1800 enrolled pupils, more than 1400 did not appear that day. Through the newspaper I had followed the progress of the School-Community Committee of P.S. 125 and now I wanted to see firsthand something of the action.

A young lady carried a sign reading, "Negotiate—don't procrastinate." I asked what the sign meant, and she answered, "For weeks we've been trying to negotiate with these officials. We want to have some way for the community to work on problems like overcrowding and obsolete facilities and curriculum and other things. Two schools are going to merge here in the fall. We even want some say in who gets chosen as principal. We need a very strong but sensitive person here. There's going to be a new building and new policies. We don't want to take over but we do think that the school people should be willing to work with us."

The student body of P.S. 125 was composed of over 50 percent black children, more than 25 percent Puerto Rican and the rest were white. Instead of attending school this day, they were to go to the West Harlem Liberation School, which was organized in a variety of buildings: the community center, St. Mary's Episcopal Church and Riverside Church. Parents, local merchants, church leaders, educators and others in the community had worked hard to bring about an operation of order, efficiency and competence. A member of the Columbia University School of

Social Work was the dean of the school. News reports had revealed remarkable spirit, cooperation and success in the movement. It appeared that the objectives of the boycott would eventually be reached and that the new style of public school administration would utilize the talents and insights of parents and others in the neighborhood who know, from within the situation, what are their children's problems and needs.

Boycotts, pickets, demonstrations, marches and vigils are almost daily news items. As pressures build up in our society, inequities persist, and public authorities entrusted with responsibilities for social planning and administration seem to drag their feet or appear to resist change, movements emerge from among the people themselves. They finally force the issues into the arena of public debate and action. Every issue imaginable has been focused in this way, including the war in Vietnam, high prices in supermarkets, the civil rights of teen-agers and racial discrimination. In some cases there have been counterpickets picketing the pickets.

Churches have not easily understood the strategies of active, conspicuous social pressure for political change. People of the church have tended to look upon community organization and other forms of radical social action with distrust and fear.

Today we see ourselves in an era abounding in experiments to find new forms of community planning and protest. Indeed, churches are themselves increasingly helping to initiate movements designed to unite persons without power to confront problems effectively.

Rochester, New York is an illustration. An organization called FIGHT has been at work since April, 1965. During the summer of 1964, Rochester was the scene of riots, events of passion and rebellion that have been repeated in many other cities since then. Perceptive persons who lived inside and outside the ghetto areas quickly found each other during the heat of those crises, drew up a list of legitimate grievances that residents had held for years and, with the help of the Industrial Areas Foundation, organized FIGHT. Its purpose was simply stated: "To provide the ghetto with voice and self-determination in urban renewal, war on poverty, law enforcement, public services, education, housing code inspection and unemployment." And churches played an important, fundamental role in that process. FIGHT's own statement indicates this: "FIGHT is a community organization representing 105 churches, fraternities, block clubs, civil rights groups, small businesses, pool halls, barbershops and youth groups in Rochester's Negro wards."

This is a dynamic movement in which power and the right to make needs felt at high levels of government and business decision-making are being claimed by people who have not had responsive channels through which they could make their feelings and demands known. The fact that it is supported heavily by church money is no small indication of an important new style of missionary activity. It is not missionary activity in the old style of zealous preaching on street corners, calling for repentance. It is missionary activity in a new sense: the church joins with secular forces of the city in an effort to act out its hope for the participation of all in a new humanity. Such hope for life is the gospel itself.

But a great price has been paid. There has been conflict. Churches have split over the issue of FIGHT's policies. Clergy and lay people have had to confront each other in angry debate. And when, in February, 1967, an open confrontation occurred between FIGHT and Rochester's principal industry, the Eastman Kodak Company, very painful battle lines became apparent throughout the entire urban area. In negotiating with the company for new open hiring practices, FIGHT had understood that an agreement with company officials had been settled. When the company announced through the press that this was not the case and cast FIGHT in a poor light, a very explosive situation erupted. It was destined to continue for many months.

The significance of this experiment in mission was described in *Christianity and Crisis* by Henry B. Clark: "The fight is on in Rochester, and the stakes are high. The most immediately involved principals are the Eastman Kodak Co. and FIGHT. . . . But the issues being joined are of critical importance for cities all over the country, and the Rochester struggle is seen as a straw in the wind by industrialists, mayors, federal officials, ecclesiastical leaders and Negroes throughout the nation. . . . This is the first major clash between a church-sponsored community organization and the church-linked power structure of an entire city. The split of clergy and laity, and the splits between and of denominations, are almost as ominous as the polarization within the community at large. We will know a lot more about the intensity of the white backlash, the sophistication of American management and the prospects for church renewal when the outcome of this struggle is clear." [1]

FIGHT, incidentally, stands for "Freedom—Integration —God—Honor—Today." It shatters the image in many minds of a tame and docile Christianity. Its notion of an angry and compassionate Jesus more nearly corresponds to the characterization of him as a revolutionary in the Italian motion picture by Pasolini, *The Gospel According to Saint Matthew.*

Now it seems that every city is the scene of many different styles of organization and social movement: councils of churches and specialized urban mission groups as well as totally new organizations composed of nonchurch members from the community. Cleveland, Ohio, for example, suffers ghettoes of black poverty and white, "hillbilly" or Appalachian misery. No one knows how many workers are trying to organize the people of the streets, but one thing is certain: some churches are involved in the middle of the action.

A separate book could be written about Chicago, which is quickly becoming an international training ground for urban ministry. Not only is the Urban Training Center developing "courses" for Protestant and Catholic workers from Canada and the United States, but the Community Renewal Society is intensifying its involvements in grass roots community organization. The Ecumenical Institute of the Church Federation of Greater Chicago is developing new styles of liturgical awareness of the forces at work in an explosive age.

Another form of racial involvement is the Mississippi Delta Ministry. An outgrowth of the great, creative explosions throughout the South during 1963, the Delta Ministry was organized by the National Council of the Churches of Christ in 1964 to carry on a positive program among the largely dispossessed Negroes in western Mississippi. This has proved to be an effective program, although often very dangerous. It has sought to organize farm workers and provide some basis of hope for the thousands left jobless there due to mechanization of the fields. Under the leadership of the late Dr. Robert Spike, the Commission on Religion and Race of the National Council of Churches has demonstrated by deeds such as this, that Christians in the church can become motivated to put their money and their bodies on the line for human freedom.

Associated with the Delta Ministry has been the Child Development Group of Mississippi, a community action project organized under the national War on Poverty legislation. Attacking problems of educational stimulation, literacy, self-esteem and opportunity for future education and work, the CDGM has run into political trouble more than once because of its relationship, on the one hand, with the Delta Ministry personnel and, on the other with workers from the Student Nonviolent Coordinating Committee (SNCC), the group of dedicated, involved black students who have effectively organized in many communities during recent years. Quite naturally, some Southern politicians have become worried about these associations in their areas of influence. It has been alleged, for instance, that the CDGM has conducted classes very much along the lines of the SNCC freedom schools of earlier days, classes in which Afro-American history and Southern problems are taught from a radical point of view.

Controversial involvements with the issues of the street, of the powerless, of the disinherited must become a part of every churchman's life. Unfortunately, the majority of church people in our society look at this kind of missionary activity with disdain. This is especially true in places where the church is expected to support "law and order," provide peace of mind and promote harmony. The concern is spreading, however, among younger people particularly, that the church has little to say and that its words accomplish next to nothing, without its engagement in the great conflicts over human rights, poverty, justice and human renewal which have remained unresolved for centuries.

This has been the case particularly in areas where more

radical groups have pressed for reforms. SNCC has become one of these. The Congress on Racial Equality has been another. Youth and adults have joined both in the name of their Christian identity. Each has a bold demand to make and different program approaches, but the central message is one of black power. Many whites have reacted to the idea of black power with indignation, as though they were surprised that Negroes would behave in such a seemingly ungrateful way. But an increasing number of church youth have picked up *The Autobiography of Malcolm X*, one of the century's great literary works about human dignity, and they have begun to hear with new ears many of the sounds coming from ghettos, from mass meetings and from spokesmen such as Stokely Carmichael and H. Rap Brown of SNCC and Floyd McKissick of CORE.

Black power has been made to mean a variety of things: hate against all white people, concentration on increasing black economic and political power in cities, increasing black voter registrations in the South, building up in Afro-Americans a new sense of pride and dignity in being black people. All of these, and many other convictions, mean much the same thing, namely, that an era in which civil rights objectives for some kind of symbolic integration of whites and blacks on white middle class terms has ended. This has given way to a new era where black people themselves are going to take charge of movements that will gain for them a share of society's benefits on their own terms.

Within the black community a wide divergence of opinion exists about how to do this. Dr. Martin Luther King, Jr. has advocated what might be called a conciliatory line of cooperation: firmness with love. Black Muslim and black nationalist groups veer off into an extreme reaction against trusting whites. The Urban League and the National Association for the Advancement of Colored People have increased efforts for legal defense funds, demonstrations of power in crisis situations and new efforts toward mutual discussion, negotiation and compromise at government and local levels.

More persons in the church are recognizing the importance of power for personal and community health, and are therefore hearing with compassion and understanding the many voices proclaiming one form of black power or another. Simply put, it means that "outsiders" (white people) may have to step aside in many situations and let the community itself organize as it desires, in the way that it desires, and adopt the platform of action it desires. In city areas this is obviously going to be difficult for many churches that shake with fear as more nonwhites move into their neighborhoods. But it is fact of life. The missionary stance of the congregation as a servant requires that the institution or the handful of individuals keep mouths shut, hear, learn the real situation and then join in or initiate action only as it seems appropriate to do so.

A statement by the Community Renewal Society provides a kind of overall summary of an ideal stance for persons, congregations and other Christian institutions:

" 'What is man?' the ancient psalmist asked, overwhelmed by the vastness of God's universe when measured against the littleness of man. Today in an urbanized world where the individuality of men can be regulated and the dignity of men eroded by despondency and dependency, those who would build a more human city still cry out, 'What is Man?'

"Yesterday our task was one of helping people for a short time until they could find employment in one of the jobs waiting for them, and start to fulfill the American dream.

In those days, the barriers were ones of language and adjustment.

"Today the barriers are far more subtle, the dream far harder to realize and our work has changed from service *for* people to programs which seek to encourage and free people to work out solutions to their own problems.

"We do not believe that the irresponsible can be commanded to be responsible citizens.

"We *do* believe that if men are encouraged and supported to speak their mind, and to organize to solve their own problems, they often become responsible independent citizens.

"We believe that 'doing for' people evokes suspicion and dependency, while trusting people to work out their own problems evokes trust and independence."

Dozens of cities on the North American continent have experienced, or will experience in the future, what the press usually calls "racial violence." Watts and Detroit have been the two most deadly upheavals during recent years in terms of persons killed, but even Waterloo, Iowa and Minneapolis have had to reckon with intensively explosive situations in black ghetto areas. One of the most important roles for people of the church to play in such an "un-cool" society is that of human interpreter.

In the words of one creative black voice: "These are not race riots. They are rebellions against a system which has continually related to the oppressed masses through channels of authority: police, schools, social workers and lawyers; or charity: church benefits, rummage sales and Christmas baskets. Violence may not be right, but it is, in most cases, the last means of communication left for a powerless people. Some people think these things are planned by professional agitators. Even Congress has de-

47

cided to legislate against so-called organizers who cross state lines. Well, let me tell you, baby, I've been through a few of them. They are out of sight, and nobody inside or outside of the ghetto has a finger on them. Most people who are black don't want them. After all, most of the deaths are black people. But look at who gets bombed: the white stores, the white-owned apartment houses and the white-dominated police cars. So, if you want to do something about these things, you've got two jobs: first, dig the unbelievable hurt and hatred in the soul of a young black, whose three-century history has been made up of castration, burnings in the night and white rapists; and second, go to work on your own 'system' of banks, schools, churches and corporations who have let this thing go on and on for so long now that almost no trust is left in the souls of the black youth."

What is the church's point of view toward rebellions in our cities and towns? The lady was terribly out of focus who wailed at a church meeting: "Our youth program seems to be failing miserably; most of the kids want to join the Peace Corps or VISTA or something like that." Well, some people have begun to take an integrated view—in the global sense—of what the protests are all about, be they small, local protests made by parent groups about situations in schools, or be they loud, sweeping, angry protests made in the name of millions of people.

As societies churn through struggles, tensions, conflicts and even violence, an immense human community of passion and commitment arises in order to do battle with the wrongs that glare unabated. The churches have now let it be known in some ways that they are interested in these dynamic movements of people. They have learned, sometimes very late in the day, that they can contribute very little that is new but quite a lot that is needed—love, support, criticism and their own bodies. This is the nature of the church's mission: to be pulled into the things of which the City of God is built.

As I stood on West 123rd Street one winter's day, chatting with people whom I'd never met before in my life and probably would never meet again, some words returned to me from a letter I received during the summer of 1964. I had been living in Oregon at the time, working with SNCC; I was their Portland contact. We had been channeling money, supplies and people to civil rights projects in the Southern states. It had been exhausting, a never-ending battle against time, against political pressures, against dropping dead for lack of sleep. Telegrams, long-distance telephone calls and special delivery letters kept us informed about the latest arrests, the latest bombings of churches or freedom houses, the latest successes in breaking down unjust laws and the latest discouragements among the workers thousands of miles away. One day a letter came from Atlanta, SNCC headquarters, which included these words: "Everyone here is so tired. It seems like we never have time even to talk to one another. And then there are all of you out there we've never met in person. It's like we're all a part of a great big church together, and all the things we do, wherever we are, are like the prayers which our mouths never get to speak."

5 Peace

On a gray misty afternoon in Prague, Czechoslovakia, a door opened on Jungmannova Street and two men and a woman walked into the cold. Wrapping their scarves and coats around them more snugly, they continued their conversation in hushed tones as together they turned down the street. At the corner stood two policemen, as though waiting for the three who approached. When they reached the corner, the police motioned to them and they stopped to speak. A moment later, they went their way, the police resuming their stroll.

Inside the small room the three had just left, a young lady

feverishly labored over her typewriter with hopes of completing the addressing job before her. Heaps of mimeographed newsletters were piled on every available table and cabinet top. As a result of the meeting that had just been held, she had even more work to do before she could go home for the night. Funds were scarce, help was at a bare minimum and only the importance of the cause propelled any of them into their work.

About a month later people in the United States and throughout the world received the mimeographed bulletin from Prague. It presented a summary of events and progress in the committee's work. It contained excerpts of recent speeches and discussions held in Prague and Bucharest. It was the Information Bulletin of the Christian Peace Conference.

The Christian Peace Conference was organized by people of the church who live in Eastern European nations: Czechoslovakia, Poland, the German Democratic Republic, Bulgaria, Rumania, Yugoslavia and the Soviet Union. Church people, professors and students, have actively worked to build up the group's program. Its primary purpose is to initiate, foster and expand conversations between Christians and Marxists in each of these societies and to make a public witness of conviction about the major issues that confront man. Unlike some "peace" groups that advocate a form of pacifism or conscientious objection, the C.P.C. stresses dialogue with decision makers in government, emphasizes human communication about issues that confront society as a whole.

It is not commonly understood on "our side" that Christians do exist in those nations on the other side of what used to be called the "Iron Curtain." In fact, the percentage of church membership in many countries is greater than that of the United States and Canada. In Czechoslovakia, for example, 75 percent of the population belongs to Roman Catholic and Protestant churches. In Poland, a traditional stronghold of Roman Catholicism, the percentage is even greater.

We are now experiencing new relaxation of East-West tensions, a disappearance of the phrase "cold war" that has for decades perpetuated a wall of misunderstanding and hostility between so-called Western and Eastern peoples. And one of the surprises for us is that, all along, Christians have been at work in all these places. In fact, in many nations, the churches have had considerable freedom to run educational programs and youth groups and maintain a rigorous life of their own. Even though governmental ideology does not encourage church affiliation, in some of the countries the state continues to finance all church expense, including pastor's salaries, building repairs and the functioning of theological seminaries. These facts may be unbelievable for persons here who have been subjected to a rather incomplete interpretation of the world situation through the press and television news media.

The Christian Peace Conference is a major, symbolic activity of Christians in Eastern European societies where the government is predominantly operated by Communist Party members. Dr. Milan Opocensky, of the Comenius Theological Faculty in Prague, asserts that party people are now admitting that Marxism has not supplied solutions for all human problems, that there are crises in human life for which Communist ideology has not found satisfying explanations. "As relationships between church and state persons are allowed to deepen among human beings, even as among friends, conversations open doorways and Christians have opportunities to express their ideas. And government officials do not automatically shut them out. In fact, sometimes they come to us for our feelings and notions about certain problems of our country or about foreign policy matters."

Dr. Opocensky reflected how one of his closest school friends, who is now a Communist Party official, attended his child's baptism service. As they stood there after the service, the friend said jokingly to Dr. Opocensky, "What will he be when he grows up, a Christian or a Marxist?" Opocensky confessed that he really could not say for certain, that his primary concern was that he be a full, responsible human being, Christian or Marxist—or by then, both.

It is important that we comprehend the complexities of this single movement of mission among some European Christians, for it points toward new directions for our own thinking. The Christian Peace Conference is a form of mission that takes seriously the given situation and commits itself to cultivating the basic humanness of it. The real question is not: how can Christians overcome and defeat Communists? The real question is: how can Christians join in the process of humanizing all elements of society by supporting the government as well as by criticizing it? Christians in Western nations have little trouble understanding the importance of supporting governments; they do not always understand the need to criticize them. In Eastern Europe we are witnessing the new stance wherein Christians do more than simply oppose the Communist Party and the Marxist ideology; Christians, indeed, are now exploring how, in the name of human good, they can appreciate and assist the efforts being made by their governments.

International peace and mutual upbuilding is now possible as it never has been in the history of mankind. The American anthropologist Margaret Mead said recently, "Do you realize that it is only in the last twenty-five years that we knew who our neighbors were? Technology is here and it has made us one people."[1]

Tim listened to the professor's opening remarks restlessly. He had been here at the university only two weeks of his freshman year and now classes were starting. In the large lecture hall were packed 800 others. He had not known what to expect and he was a little overwhelmed by the hugeness of the place and the impersonal rush of his schedule. And he had not known fully why he had come, except that he had assumed that this was the next step for him toward whatever it was that he was supposed to start doing in life.

"Let's assume, for the moment, that we are all interested in the future existence of mankind on this planet. I use the phrase, *'for the moment'* quite on purpose, because I don't assume that everyone here *is* vitally interested in man's future—that is to say, the future of the total family of man, the species *homo sapiens*. I don't even want to discuss whether or not we all *ought* to be so dedicated or *can* be vitally concerned. All I ask is that we agree to ponder together what the problems of humanity are as though we were really interested in them, *for the moment.*"

The professor obviously had his own doubts about who was there and why. This was a time in which adults could not assume too much about youth. Everything had to be tentative, put in simple words that spell it out clearly. "He's right," Tim thought to himself, as the speaker's voice droned on through the first point of the lecture. "I'm not completely sure that I'm interested in what happens to the species *homo sapiens.* I'm mostly interested in what happens to me. That's a big enough worry. I could hardly handle that, let alone consider the future of the world. What do I know about international issues? What can I do about them anyway, one person against the whole mess?"

And Tim doodled on his note paper during the rest of the lecture period. As one of the nation's "experts" outlined his concerns about the great issues that confront mankind, Tim and many other students in the crowded classroom recorded race cars, girls, abstract designs and phrases. "Frodo lives." "If it moves, fondle it." "I'd like you to get to know me better." It was the button era of history.

Tim listened to the chaplain's sermon with the same restlessness he felt the other day during the lecture. He was not sure why he was sitting here in chapel, except out of habit. He had been a "church type," a youth fellowship officer and all the rest. He had done his bit for God and country through his local church.

"As Christians, we are called to a mission. We are called to give ourselves *in* mission for the sake of the world and its illnesses. The word 'mission,' you know, comes from the same root as 'missile.' They both have to do with something that is thrown or hurled into space. The American planes that fly over North Vietnam are on call to complete a specified number of 'missions' every day. Christians are called to see themselves under this kind of obligation—to consider themselves *in mission* in a world that is desperately in need of the gospel of Jesus Christ."

He turned off the sermon even more quickly than the professor's lecture. At least the professor had the courtesy to assume there was no obligation on anybody's part to be concerned about what was happening in the world. The chaplain, on the other hand, was laying it all down in so many words. He was pronouncing what God expected of all Christians. He was making a demand that people like Tim should feel a deep concern for the state of people in need. This kind of talk got nowhere with Tim now. A few months ago it might have stirred up some feelings of guilt in him, or it might even have moved him to where he wanted to do something—like write a letter to his congressman or give money for a CARE package. But he didn't feel these things now.

Tim didn't doodle in the chapel. One doesn't doodle in chapels. He simple stared straight at the chaplain, in the pulpit high above him, his mind darting quickly back to those fabulous moments during the summer. There were terrific beach scenes, magnificent moments with Charlene, wild times with his new Mustang, much good dancing. Even the job in the packing plant had gone well, with an easy boss and a bunch of clowns to work with. He had gotten to swim every day and his body was in great shape. And by the end of the summer he had enough loot to stock up with clothes for school. "Amen." Tim stood with the congregation as it sang, *Now Thank We All Our God.*

Tim listened to the bull session with keen interest. It was very late but the dormitory was wide awake. Tim had heard about dorm life and was excited by this freedom to stay up and wander around all night if he pleased. People were always arguing or joking or pulling off great gags —or talking about ideas. As Tim listened to Bud and Charlie go at each other about world problems, his mind wandered very little, and when it did, only to recall some of the bits of the past week—parts of the professor's lecture and the chaplain's sermon. He tried to match them all up. "Canada is wrong when it sends wheat to Red China. All it's doing is feeding our enemies. Anybody who buddies up with them Commies is helping out the other side."

"But people are starving over there. You're not against sending food to India, are you?"

"So long as they support our policy against the Communists. You can never tell about India. They're shifty. They'll never come right out and say where they stand."

"That's right, and it just happens that Russia sends food and other kinds of help to the Indians."

"Look, there are only three different kinds of countries in the world: us and our friends who stand behind us as we protect democracy, our enemies who are trying to take over the world, and those so-called neutral or uncommitted ones who need our nudging so that they see our side of it and back us up."

"No, no, no. You're looking at it like a Western movie— good guys, bad guys and townspeople. That's nonsense. Communists are different now. You can't talk about them as though they were all alike. The Chinese are one thing and the Russians are very different. Look at how they fight each other. And the Czechs and Yugoslavs and Rumanians are all becoming more independent of Russia, and everything is open now. They really are human beings, you know."

"Well, if you get sentimental about it, sure. They're human beings. So what? When a guy comes at you with a gun, what do you think?—well, here comes a human being; I'll shake his hand if he doesn't blow my head off first?"

57

No one was on the same wave length. The professor's ideas were very sound and well expressed. He cautiously and patiently developed them without requiring that anyone agree with him or believe him. It had been an intellectual exercise "for the moment." The chaplain's words, on the other hand, comprised a call to duty, a series of marching orders for Christians. They, too, were clearly developed, but they required response, commitment to a whole way of thinking and acting. Charlie and Bud, now arguing partly out of emotional feeling and partly out of ignorant conviction, seemed to care little about what anyone thought at all. Neither presented an ordered case and neither gave orders. Here was a clash of feelings that meant something to two people. It was really a clash of two people. Each injected himself into the battle.

Tim wondered if anything that he had heard could be trusted. None of it reached his guts, where he felt things strongly, where his vivid memories of Charlene lived, where his love for the water and his delight in the beat lived. Everyone, including the President of the United States, was telling Tim that he must be concerned about people less fortunate than himself and that he must do something that promotes world brotherhood. But no one had reached his deep feelings with a reason why he should care, why he should change everything just to help out needy people, or why he should even think about it.

The World Conference on Church and Society convened in Geneva, Switzerland, July 12-26, 1966. It attempted to confront the questions raised by people like Tim—why should Christians respond to world issues? Christian participants from every region in the world discussed their insights with one another. It was a revealing and explosive meeting.

The speech of Mr. 'Bolga Ige, a Nigerian lawyer and an Anglican, was illustrative of the penetrating search for truth. He awakened the whole conference by such remarks as these:

The countries of Africa, Asia, and Latin America have not sought to be free from colonial rule simply because they dislike the usually pink faces of their colonial masters; nor because they want freedom in the abstract. . . . The main reason we wanted to be free was so we could build our nations in the way we wanted, and not in the way our colonial masters thought we would or should want. We demanded our inalienable right to be free to organize our own lives in the way that would make us truly man; to create new weapons that would break the mental and cultural shackles that had bound us in the past; to create new opportunities which we never had but which we have been taught and which we now know will give confidence, courage, and strength to our children and to our children's children; to organize our trade and relationships so that our ordinary people eat well and if possible put something by from the sweat of our brows; to build new nations where man shall no longer be haunted by fear of other men. . . .

Mr. Ige continued his passionate statement by saying,

The new nations had hardly been born before they were thrown into the turbulent sea of ideological confrontations. The Communist worldview of the ultimate triumph of socialism is equated with Soviet hegemony, and the United States of America believes that it must direct its efforts against this "pernicious" thing, not so much (as it says) for its own safety as for the salvation of all mankind in the fold of 'free nations.' Both these countries are powerful and between them they can destroy this world with nuclear war. . . .

It would have been all right if these giant nations stayed in their own countries and merely thundered from there. No. Then they came breathing down the necks of the new nations.

Because of their material wealth they dazzle the eyes of the new nations, and many of them have at one time or another, had to practice political harlotry. All of the new nations, one would say—except Communist China. . . .

For there can be no peace in the world where two-thirds of mankind are patronizingly referred to as 'the poor,' 'the under-developed,' 'the third world,' and now 'the newly awakened peoples.' There can be no peace in the world where seventy-five nations have their economic (and therefore their political) future dictated by the narrow self-interest of Europe and America. There can be no peace where the Soviet Union and the United States arrogate to themselves the monopoly of directing the future of the world and of other nations. . . .

And so, what do the nations have to look at now, as that which symbolizes the best among themselves; they have the Chinese People's Republic—nationalist, militant, economically free and at the same time unyielding in its commitment for the freedom and full emancipation of the nations of Africa, Asia and Latin America.[2]

Such stinging words remind us that we live among a minority people even though our society produces most of the wealth of the world and exercises a great amount of power.

All of these messages are getting through to the denominations. So-called foreign missions have been fundamentally reevaluated by churches. The image of an earlier day of the lonely preaching missionary who went about in the jungle with a Bible in hand is forever dead. Few major denominations commission and send any such people overseas. In most cases, the preaching and teaching of Christian faith is assumed by people of the country itself. Indigenous church bodies are now in charge, whether the locale be Nigeria, India, Japan, Brazil or any other nation. Evangelism, pastoral work and educational ministries are the enterprise of Christians who live and work in terms of their own society and who know what the twentieth century is in the perspective of their own people.

When American, Canadian, British or other Western churches send personnel overseas, it is more often by invitation of groups in the other country. And these persons are increasingly specialized. Doctors, nurses, teachers, agriculturalists, scientists and others with special skills are asked for, and sent to work in church-related institutions or even government-run schools and hospitals. When the Peace Corps was organized just a few years ago, many consultations were held with church mission officials whose advice was valued because of their long experience in programs of overseas technical and material assistance. And the Peace Corps pattern has reflected most of the strong points of enlightened mission work.

But Mr. Ige's remarks point out the need for a new era for world missionary efforts. Many governments in Asia and Africa are now discouraging or excluding Christian missionaries from other countries. For one thing, they are a nuisance. They implant ideas in the minds of people that some governments find threatening or unsettling. The presence of these people, even though they contribute to the life of the culture, exposes the inadequacies of the nation's customs or the injustices of the regime.

What is more, the missionaries themselves quite often fail to understand the revolutions taking place all around them. For example, an American worker in Ghana will often assume that his fellow workers should be striving for American-type goals for the society and standards for personal conduct. There is an implicit American value system in operation in all that the missionary does, and it is communicated every time he turns around. The motion picture, *Hawaii*, while it does not present a balanced view, makes a rather devastating judgment against such transplanting of foreign ideas. And now that new governments are creating new nations, as Mr. Ige points out, the paternalizing spirit of foreign personnel, particularly people from one of the large, powerful nations of the world, is an obstacle for which the leaders of these new societies have little or no tolerance.

What does the world situation demand at the moment? Does it seem to be an essential thing that Christians convert non-Christians into Christians? Or does it not seem to be more critical that such issues as starvation, ignorance, disease and population control be faced by everybody? What can the Church say to someone like Tim, who says that he has enough to do if he tries to settle his own life's problems?

It is very simple, really. Christians in affluent nations must learn how to think, feel and respond to the day's news as "global humans." Now that mass media have opened the way for instantaneous information, Christians must develop a style of awareness, of information-gathering, that puts them into touch with events everywhere, and an accompanying style of response on the strictly human level. "People are being bombed in Vietnam. They are starving in China. They are dying in the Congo. They are all my brothers."

Certain activities are already producing increased world consciousness among some affluent Christians. The number of overseas student exchange programs multiplies every year. Churches are expending an increased share of their energies through such channels as the International Christian Youth Exchange and other programs that put people into different cultural situations. The Peace Corps has become an important arm of mission for young people, just as has VISTA, the domestic version of the same program. The Experiment in International Living provides yet another bridge. Youth hostels encircle the world, and the Council on Student Travel has never been more active. Many universities operate campuses overseas which students attend for at least a year of their regular academic program.

The traditional avenues of service overseas, such as work camps, the program of Ecumenical Voluntary Service and other international agencies in which churches participate, are now reflecting a broadened sensitivity to the political and economic revolutions of other continents. It is no longer safe for a Western Christian to jump into an international service program where he or she will have to work alongside persons from other nations. His ideas will be put through the most rigorous challenges. Quite often, however, he or she will emerge much more a "global human" than before.

The international, global perspective is basic to any discussion of the church's mission. We cannot be Christian without being global. Anything less than that is subject to the pretty nationalistic, locally-determined bags in which we live. We must start with the proposition that the bags we inhabit are not the total realities about the world and then spend the rest of our lives fighting our way out of them.

Mao Tse-tung has written: "How should we judge whether a youth is a revolutionary? How can we tell? There can only be one criterion, namely, whether or not he is willing to integrate himself with the broad masses of workers and peasants and does so in practice. If he is willing to do so and actually does so, he is a revolutionary;

otherwise he is a non-revolutionary or a counter-revolutionary." [3]

Mao's call to mission may sound impossible to follow, but it is not unlike the Christian call to mission. Christ, "the man for others," advocated that one "integrate himself with the broad masses and peasants" in all that one does. His emphasis on the physical, total human self of persons differs from Mao's only in one respect: implicit in the Communist call is a demand for conformity to a peculiar, social doctrine produced by Mao himself. But the call to the Christian is no less absolute in its requirements that one conform to the idea of global humanity, that one commit oneself to all programs, all policies, all actions and all engagements which overcome the separations, the barriers and the hostilities of a fragmented world.

6 Personhood

All pacifists are sex perverts," read the headline of a national publication on the newsstand. I didn't buy a copy.

"I think there's truth in that," said a man who happened to be in my office a few hours later. "I've had my doubts about all these peaceniks—beards, long hair, free love and all that. Besides, the UN is just a Communist wedge into the morale of America, you know. I agree with the saying, 'Get the U.S. out of the UN and the UN out of the U.S.' U Thant has no business going around the world sticking his nose into our stand in Vietnam. Anyway, they'll get sent up eventually."

"Who'll get sent up eventually?" I asked, puzzled by the speaker's abrupt changes of subject.

"All those perverts," he answered.

"You mean the pacifists?"

He nodded. "They're silly fools. They haven't thought a minute about what they're doing. They aren't worthy of the name Christian or American. They haven't studied the facts. They haven't looked into the real problems. They're dupes of the communists."

Luckily he went away after a few minutes. But then I went through my mail and found a copy of a conservative group's publication in which the United Church of Christ was being blasted for its ministry with homosexuals in San Francisco. It had been written up in *Newsweek* a few weeks earlier. Now the right-wingers were really taking us to task about our own sexual morality. All I needed to complete my day was for someone, anyone, male or female, to walk through the door in the nude.

But all of this hurt me. Having been the pastor of a parish, I had been involved with people in nearly every kind of personal crisis imaginable including suicide, incest, rape, homosexuality, attempted murder and bomb threats. When you are inside a situation with a live human being, your guts get informed even when your mind doesn't. And it's hard to put feelings into words, and so you don't talk very much about intimate things with other people—except when you're forced to.

I've noticed that I'm increasingly forced to—that is, personal crises, personal problems, have become the center of public controversy more than ever before. In a pressure cooker society in which masses of people are forced into a single form of confinement side by side, no matter what the weather, the individual desire or private preference, the behavior of individuals who "deviate" from the conspicuous norms is glaring, easily detectable and immediately judged, not to say condemned. And now, as never before, the church has been called upon to enter into the public debates about private morality.

Many fascinating ministries have been developed in our day. Often these are not to the liking of more conservative members of churches, but much to the delight of a population that has been waiting for churches to become compassionately identified with persons who have special problems and needs.

The Rev. Rick Mawson spends all his time in the gambling and other recreational establishments of the Las Vegas strip in Nevada. He has no parish in the ordinary sense. He has formed trusting relationships, sometimes friendships with gamblers, vacationers, prostitutes, entertainers and others who flock to or earn their living from the Las Vegas brand of leisure culture. Rick brings no judgmental presuppositions to his relationships with persons. He literally "floats" around, being where people are, bringing a presence into the situation, not of the "official" religiosity of the church but of the love and concern for persons that Jesus continually described as a no-strings-attached kind of giving.

Rick Mawson's ministry is underwritten by several denominational and local churches, although he himself has no formal responsibilities in an organized congregation. He may lead or be part of some kind of worship activity in a motel or other setting as the legitimate need arises, but he rarely lets himself become identified with the relatively uninviting image of formal religion. He has been seen in a clerical collar. Everybody knows who he is. But he is free to just be around, to simply exist as an ear and an eye and a nose, rather than a mouth—as one who cares about what happens to people who get hung up with one kind of panic or another.

Rick Mawson once even suggested that money be provided for babysitters' fees paid out by prostitute mothers while they had to be away from home "working." That suggestion produced raised eyebrows in certain quarters of the church. Without condoning prostitution in any way, we can certainly understand what Rick has tried to convey through such an insight and we can perceive the depth of his dedication to a radical form of what might best be called a personal, pastoral ministry of presence.

The phrase "ministry of presence" was the key idea among the clergy and laity who spent hours every night on Hollywood's Sunset Strip during the fall and winter of 1966-67. When swarms of young adults and teenagers began to crowd the sidewalks creating problems for certain proprietors whose businesses catered to a "clean cut" kind of young person, county and city police moved in to clear away all the others. Because of the police methods and their own expressed objectives, the young people rebelled with force. Violation of the curfew law, for example, was cited as one of the central issues, even though young adults dressed in coats and ties or dresses were not picked up after hours. The so-called hippies' beards, long hair, strange clothing and unorthodox mannerisms were conspicuous targets. Immediately, certain establishments, such as Pandora's Box, which had been meeting places for the young people, were closed up or patrolled heavily by armed officers.

During the period of a few nights in November, 1966, more than five hundred arrests were made on Sunset Strip during protest rallies, walks and other demonstrations by youth on Sunset Boulevard. The youth themselves had mobilized an all-out attack on the city and county officials for becoming "pawns of unscrupulous real estate interests" who wanted a certain exclusive image for Sunset Strip and therefore wanted "undesirables" cleared out of the area. During the picketing and protesting, which even *The New York Times* described as orderly, the police literally "wiped them out."

A few—too few—clergy of several denominations had been ready for this confrontation weeks before it happened. The Rev. Ross Greek of the West Hollywood Presbyterian Church, whose building is on Sunset Boulevard, had been warning everybody of the growing discontent among the youth and the establishment owners who sided with them. He himself believed in their rights to be around the Strip area, but he knew that most adults there harbored real hostilities against the young people. When the explosion occurred, Ross Greek addressed the Hollywood Chamber of Commerce. What he said could well provide a kind of manifesto, in spirit, for sensitive churches concerned with youth.

"I know, respect and admire your many wonderful accomplishments," he began. "You are astute businessmen, civic leaders and generous donors to many noteworthy causes. May I invite you to listen to what these youth are saying to us. They are challenging us to think through ways of meeting our responsibility to show concern for them. They are saying: First, accept us as valid human beings! Don't bug us. We are no more kooks than the Dodger fans who wear crazy hats and wave pennants for the home team. (We don't even make noise—and certainly don't yell, 'Kill the Umpire!') We want to live by love. Second, we who are referred to as 'long hairs' are declaring our rights to dress as we choose . . . and dance odd dances. Third, we believe the 'curfew' is unfair to us. It is the responsibility of our parents—not the city or county—to determine when we shall be home. . . ."

More than thirty other Protestant clergymen "heard" what the youth were saying to the society as a whole and they delegated some of their number to represent them before official bodies, including the county commissioners. And they themselves, together with lay people of all denominations, began to spend time along the Strip, in the coffeehouses, restaurants and on the streets, simply listening to what was happening. Their ministry was one of "presence," vital interest and concern, not judgment or moralizing. And due to their rapid and genuine involvement on the Strip, the young people seemed to welcome them "to the fold" with what Paul Kittlaus called "a kind of rejoicing." The church had been willing to come to them in terms of their own crises rather than in terms of its own presuppositions.

Fortunately, the work of those churchmen seems to have caught hold. The West Hollywood Presbyterian Church voted to dissolve as a formal congregation and make its entire building available for programs by, for and with the youth of the Strip. Ross Greek, the former pastor, remains as director of these new forms of ministry. Former members of the congregation remain as workers in the various forms of work which make up the total program. Ross Greek describes a program of counseling with youth who have left home, persons who have contracted venereal disease, homosexual males and females, pregnant girls and suicidal individuals.

Furthermore, on the level of political action, the Joint Action in Mission group, composed of urban church executives and others from several denominations, continues to "represent" the youth before legislative, enforcement and policy making bodies of government, civic affairs and business groups. John Hamilton, one of the student leaders, is now working with this and another group in a research effort to probe the complex problems of the Strip. The slow, painful process of adjustment, interpretation and eventual communication among all of the interests involved has begun. It will take time.

As I sat at my desk in the wake of my deviant-hating acquaintance, staring at the right-wing broadside against the church's getting mixed up with society's "unlovables," a staff colleague entered with *Essence,* a college literary magazine. I opened it and this poem jumped out:

> *I don't want to go to church*
> *To hear a mimeographed minister*
> *Tell a microphone about the building fund*
> *In a humming, immaculate auditorium*
> *That assures weather-free worship.*
>
> *I tire of hearing abstract rites*
> *Bouncing off painted windowpanes*
> *To be then soaked up by thick*
> *Plush carpets which are soil-free and sterile.*
>
> *Let me take over the church.*
> *I promise to smash the windows,*
> *Tear down the doors and fling dirt*
> *All over the congregation and floor,*
> *Then plant a seed in the rotting carpet.*[1]

It occurred to me that what this poem says is precisely what is needed and happening and what is feared, a revolution within churches, a turnabout in favor of human life issues. It is needed because the mission of the church is to serve others without asking anything in return. It is feared because the church as an institution reacts to radical changes as any institution does—it is slow to comprehend needs and ways to meet them. The poet describes the way many individuals feel about churches that have shut them out because of their strange or startling circumstances.

What happened to one pastor in the western plains has occurred in countless congregations. A lovely girl of his church, a choir member and a popular member of the youth group, became pregnant. Suddenly a chill came over the place when she walked in. As a result, she walked out, convinced that she was no longer good enough for the church. The personal presence of the pastor and a few others in her life served, however, to convey love and caring to her. But her experience has been repeated so many times in so many different ways elsewhere that it's easy to understand why a large segment of population no longer considers the church a truly sensitive, open movement of love and honesty and integrity. Rather, while its image continues to consist of self-centered comforts, class and race consciousness, "good guy" hypocrisy, more people are identifying with other forms of "love" activity—be-ins, peace movements, the arts—whose expressed purpose is to *live* love.

This is why the Glide Foundation in San Francisco, a group endowed originally by funds from Methodist Church sources but now increasingly ecumenical, actively supports a presence with homosexual persons, "free men," anti-war demonstrators and other "deviants," as well as with "normal" people. Trying to let human relationships grow in an environment totally apart from the realm of value judgments, moral codes and tastes is a nearly impossible task. It is, however, a crucial idea for Christians to understand and act upon. Christianity is not primarily a set of rules; it is a movement of persons who feel glad about and responsible for life.

The involvement of Christians in the Council on Religion and Homosexuality, therefore, does not assume that young men and women who are homosexual will, as a result of the Council's activities, decide to cease being homosexual. The Christian mission is not a matter of wishing people were something other than what they are. It is a matter of taking people seriously as they are at the moment, as human beings, loving them with respect, appreciating their dignity as brothers. "Christians can bring no superior influence or insight to others," says a member of the Council. "They can bring their own sense of freedom from fear and their urgency about justice, and they can talk about themselves, when it's natural and fitting for them to do so." And this is the basis on which relationships are built.

Homosexuals face intense problems in our culture. If they are male, in most places their sexual relationships are forbidden by law. They can receive sentences of up to sixty years in prison. Furthermore, they are excluded from jobs by many employers, including the Federal Government. If they are female, little or no attention is paid them. Thus, a strange double standard about sex continues to operate in our culture.

"Homophile organizations," such as the Mattachine Society and the Janus Society, have been organized not to promote homosexuality but to work for a change in laws and a relaxation of public anxiety about people who are homosexuals. Should two persons of legal age be allowed to live by mutual consent with one another in total intimate

73

sharing? Our society is divided in its opinion but at the same time it has *not* faced this question squarely, and in such forms of dialogue as those of the Council on Religion and Homosexuality, Christians are participating in a serious, enlightened search for ways to communicate the concern and the immediate need for change in laws and attitudes. Already Great Britain's Parliament has made striking changes in English law to this effect. The Council hopes to push for a level of maturity in our culture similar to some of the cultures of Europe, where homosexuality is often accepted without hysteria.

In short, rather than do as the society does—consider homosexuality as a sickness and nothing more—Christian participants in groups like the Council and other forms of direct, personal relationship with homosexual persons are willing and ready to accept homosexuality as another of many human circumstances. Although a Christian case for heterosexuality may be in the back of our minds—that is, a preference for full human sexual expression in the marriage of male and female—we can no longer, if indeed we ever could, insist that all human beings *can* or *must* fulfill our expectations. And when they do not, we have no right to consider them inferior or subhuman. None of us is free from imperfections; all of us can accept each other as is. The New Testament calls this idea *grace*.

This is always a hallmark of Christian mission, and we see it at work now in the midst of countless other battles having to do with the personhood of others.

The struggle for liberalizing abortion laws is now gathering full steam. In nearly every state, as well as on the national level, there exists an association of lawyers, clergy, educators, psychiatrists and others who are working for radical changes in the legal status of abortion. Why, for example, should a sixteen-year-old girl who has been raped be forced to give birth to a child conceived in such an act of violence? Should a woman who, in the opinion of qualified medical examiners, faces a complete mental collapse have no right to decide about an unwanted pregnancy, which might shove her across the line of sanity? Should feebleminded, poor or incurably diseased women be forced to give birth to children once they are pregnant? Who suffers the most—society, the child or the mother? When is a human fetus a living being with rights of its own which, when denied it, make one guilty of murder?

The questions point to complex and moving human issues. Most Roman Catholics and Protestants differ widely on most of them at the present moment. But the movement is now afoot toward a radical call for revisions of laws and a complete change of attitude.

The National Young Adult Project, begun by The Methodist Church and now joined by other denominations, has drawn resources and competent persons together for concentration in large urban areas, increasingly the living centers of single persons, eighteen to thirty-five. Many young adults who live in cities face the most terrifying loneliness, and in their search for identity and some form of supporting community they experience all of the extremes—from ecstatic, recreational sex, to morbid, empty, suicidal depression. Who is going to mobilize communities of concern for detached young adults who lose themselves in the jungles of big cities? The National Young Adult Project is pushing ahead through experiments in a few selected cities, hoping to branch out into all major urban centers with integrated ministries that transcend religious, class, racial and age barriers.

What about marijuana and LSD? Now that they are

spreading in use, do more stringent laws solve the human problems involved? In some areas, campus ministers and ministers in inner city parishes are openly calling for a rational response to drugs and marijuana. Dr. Arthur Alderstein, a psychology professor at Rutgers University, summed up an attitude of caution before a group of college deans and guidance counselors:

"Education rather than suppression and support rather than expulsion are the means educators should use to counteract the harmful aspects of drug use. . . . I want to be in the position of helping students who have become potheads. It seems to me that there is but one caveat: never put the good image of the institution above the welfare of the students." This is an attitude basic to the ministries now expanding among high school youth, as well as college students. But it is hardly off the ground in most churches. It must be started somehow.

The death penalty has been abolished in several states. Church support and leadership has proved essential in every case. Church people have worked either through special action groups composed of persons from a variety of backgrounds and disciplines or through groups within the church.

Sexual problems, free speech, electronic eavesdropping, the draft, technological and scientific breakthroughs, divorce, mass media, big business; these are but a few of the other urgent human intersections of life about which thousands of pages have been written and around which creative persons in the church have begun to respond through new, experimental kinds of study, dialogue, action and interpretation.

In some cases, clergy have become detached from congregations for service in specific settings: night ministries on the street, industrial ministries in factories and among corporation officials, street work with gangs, institutional work among the elderly, tutoring among migrants, organizing agricultural laborers. In some cases they have left recognizable church structures to exercise a ministry through another organization—the War on Poverty, peace groups, civil rights organizations, publishing, radio and television, the arts.

Lay persons in churches have begun to understand how their everyday commitments, through occupation and personal interest, are indeed forms of personal mission. An architect who runs a weekend coffeehouse in Milwaukee, a lawyer who runs for mayor in Portland, Oregon, a housewife who makes her home a kind of drop-in center for youth in Lexington, Massachusetts, a high school principal who marches for peace in Pennsylvania, a truck driver in Calgary who works with "hard-core" youth on their cars, have in common an understanding of mission as having a personal stake in what happens to other people, regardless of who they are. Out of religious motivation, such individuals plunge themselves into the secular fray precisely because they are interested in mission to and for the sake of the world and the people in it.

The uniqueness of the Christian's involvement is difficult to pinpoint, but it is surely to be found, in part, in the totality and depth of motivation, which springs from the Bible. A group of persons organized recently to be with the night people of their town, a small city beset with dope, prostitution, unfaithful wives or husbands, upper- or middle-class senior and junior executives who stretch a martini lunch into the wee morning hours. They called themselves Night Watch. After a period of breaking in they found themselves involved with people attempting suicide and grieving over personal calamities, a town's leading dope pusher asked some of them to protect him against some foes who had threatened his life, and a man ready to gun down someone else let himself be talked out of it by one of them. A bar owner called them in recently for help in stopping a fight, and he later explained, "These guys aren't holding tent meetings, you know. They're here to listen —just listen." Something unique has come through these persons that other agencies and professionals have not yet provided. Is it sincerity, commitment—or something else, perhaps the height and depth, length and breadth of their orientation as Christians?

The theological reflections of some of the members of the group shed light on this. Episcopalian William Boli said, "Jesus was concerned with the whole person, not merely the soul. We must be too." LaVern Franzen, Missouri Synod Lutheran, said, "The church must demonstrate the concern it says it had. There's need for reconciliation and healing beyond pulpit and pew. Ours is not the offbeat ministry it's often pictured to be, but an exciting and refreshing way to cut artificial activities and to sit with people where they sit. Jesus did a lot of that himself." Alvin D. Rockey, a pastor of the Church of God in North America, said, "As a Night Watcher I lose myself in the needs of others. It's a great privilege being born anew. It means a lot to be the instrument through which the redeeming power of God flows to others." Roman Catholic priest Joseph Schabel said, "I was spending most of my time saving the saved. Christ spent most of his time with sinners and publicans. Now I realize that my presence as a clergyman is saying something—saying God still loves this man or woman . . . God has not forgotten . . . they are important."[2]

These remarks are actually theological reflections because

each of the men who made them has tried to relate his identity in Christian tradition with the specifics of the moment in which he is living. That is what theology is—a form of perceiving what is going on now through the eyes of one's religious heritage.

In its most creative forms, theological reflection is exciting. The Night Watch men, for example, have taken the plunge into action. They have gotten involved over their heads, simply because they have felt deeply about the lonely people who roam their town at night. After entering the fray, however, they have been able to articulate how all of this makes sense in terms of their Christian comprehension of realities in the world. Each of them is making a profound statement of what he believes about God's activity, Jesus' real mission, what love is, reconciliation, the church's role in the world and the inherent dignity and sanctity of human beings.

Their theological words are unimportant, really. To the man on the street, words are less important than bodily expressions of commitment—physical presence. These things really "preach the word" of the gospel, the good news.

But theological reflection is important for people in the church. It is the only way we have of keeping our bearings. The Biblical heritage out of which we have sprung is the record of our spiritual and cultural ancestors. It contains the seeds, the basic ideas, around which we gather and because of which we scatter as a committed community. It presents a view of human existence in the world that we still find to be important. It sets before us the words of prophets and apostles that, when heard by us in terms of their predicaments, may make some new sense to us in this fragment of time in history.

Biblical literature contains a wild assortment of poetic

interpretations of history, and although we are not usually required to believe in any of them literally, they vibrate with other kinds of truth and must be taken more seriously than empirical documentation. And for persons in the church engaged in the chaos of the twentieth- twenty-first century epoch, it is necessary more than ever that theological reflection be attempted, earnest efforts to keep track of where we've been and where we're headed, so that we may gain some idea of where we are.

This is precisely what some artists have done with the Bible. Even though they are not particularly fond of the church, they explore biblical ideas. Albert Camus, one of the greatest atheist existentialists of this century, born a Roman Catholic only to bolt from it later in life, kept returning to Christian ideas for his raw material. One of the reasons for this, he explained, was his understanding of how the early characters in the Judeo-Christian culture loved life in time so much, and how clearly they seemed to know how to act out their decisions. This, said he, was a basic existential idea, one of immediate response to concrete situations. While he became an enemy of organized religion, he nonetheless maintained his devotion to the great themes of the Judeo-Christian tradition because they kept clear for him some of the important human values that transcend time and have universal significance.

Without a continual probing of this heritage, we easily fall into ruts of all sorts. We become absorbed by the heat and pressure of the activities around us. We get tightly enclosed in our bags. The biblical word provides the openings, the judgments, the correctives, the new challenges to our egos. Just as we become almost convinced that we are good guys, we had best run to someone who will read to us something by Jesus, Amos or Isaiah, lest we become idolatrous of the thing we're on at the moment. Theological reflection is more important for new forms of missionary activity today than it ever has been.

In other words, if it were to be proven true somehow that "all pacifists are sex perverts," one of these thinking missionaries would immediately respond with something like: "So what! Who isn't a pervert of some kind? Name me a single normal person! Speak up! I can't hear you! Can't you name me a single normal person? So what is normal?" That is the basis for authentic Christian mission in the personal, human sense.

Jesus is certainly the clarifying symbol for us when we search for standards. His ministry drew so much flak because of his refusal to pigeonhole people according to their caste, their morality, their political convictions, their cleanliness and their religiosity. He was never silent when it came to moral and ethical considerations. But his real value system could be seen only through the way he treated other human beings. His own personal standards were carved out of his belief and his experience. He never coerced others into swallowing his line. They were free, as in the case of the rich young man, to walk away from him. Jesus never ran after them. They had made their decision by themselves and for themselves; let them live by it. God bless them. So he went around with "loose" women, he would not wave away unwashed, longhaired beggars and he befriended a thief even while he was hanging on the cross. Nothing put off Jesus. He was wired in perfectly to every situation. He felt the soul of the moment. That was right where it was at that time, and that is right where it's at today.

7 Congregations

The roof leaks. The furnace has been out of commission for two months. Several windows are cracked or broken. In the dead of winter, these conditions pose problems. The pews have collected rolls of dirt and droppings of plaster. The carpeting is crumpled and caked with mud from little boys playing tag during Sunday school.

By 9:30 A.M. Sunday, church school classes are in session. Children and young people are crammed into too-small rooms with electric heaters. A spirit of temporary emergency is in the air and everyone treats it all as a game to be played.

By 10:30 A.M., the pastor, an organist and an usher are putting the old meeting room in order for morning service. Heated by the stoves in the adjoining kitchen, this space is barely big enough for the sixty-odd people who still turn out for "church" in spite of the condition of the building. The chairs are arranged along three sides of a rectangle, an altar sitting at the open end.

At 11:00 A.M., people have begun to fill up the last rows first; the "choir," a shadow of its former self, occupies a section near the piano, and the prelude begins. Some minutes later the pastor opens the worship service. A hymn is sung, prayers are recited, Scripture is read and at 11:25 A.M. announcements are given.

"Be sure to remember that the ladies will meet on Tuesday for lunch and a program on overseas missions. The church board will meet Tuesday night for its monthly meeting. The membership class will meet in the pastor's study on Saturday morning. Bible study group meets at the home of Mrs. Brown on Wednesday afternoon. Choir practices on Thursday evening and we urge anyone who likes to sing to come. The young people will meet tonight for a film on sexual morality. Any persons who wish to go to the Council of Churches annual dinner meeting are asked to make reservations with Mrs. Simpson before Friday noon. The clothing drive concludes in two weeks, so make sure you bring your donations and put them in the clothing barrel. Persons who desire to dedicate memorial flowers on Easter Sunday are asked to bring them to the church at least one hour before the service begins. Tickets for the pancake supper presented by the young people go on sale next week."

After a long pastoral prayer, the choir sings, a hymn is sung, the pastor preaches and the offering is taken. After

83

another prayer, the closing hymn is sung and the benediction given. It is 12:05 and people file out. The atmosphere is anything but cheery. Even though the people have been sitting near each other they behave as though a great distance separated most of them.

Mumblings can be heard near the outside door about what Easter will be like. Without a sanctuary and an organ, how can we have an Easter service? Won't the denomination be willing to advance money to us for our building repairs so that we can resume our regular worship services? Every week in that old meeting room makes us long for the beauty of the regular ways! If we don't get back into the sanctuary soon we'll lose all our members.

It is a nippy winter's day outside. The people scurry off to their cars. The grey stone church building looks desolate and forlorn, huddled among the houses of the crowded neighborhood. The community is made up of Italian, German and recently arrived Afro-Americans. They do not mix well. They are hostile about their racial differences, their class differences and their religious differences. Poverty has engulfed more than half of the residents, crime and delinquency are on the increase, housing and employment inequities discourage most of the black people and tensions are high, even during the winter, when people stay indoors as much as they can.

The membership of this congregation is now about half black. The parish traditionally has been a German one. Hardly any youth, black or white, show interest in the church, even though the pastor has encouraged them to do new, imaginative things in drama and music. Many of the lower income black people of the neighborhood appreciate the pastor's commitment and sensitivity, but they do not feel welcome in the congregation's activities.

The decrepit building has forced the issue on all of them. What is our reason for maintaining a congregation in this place? What is our mission? Can we say that we know what mission is? Should we repair the building and resume business as usual, or would it be better to disband and turn the building over to someone else? The questions are painful ones, and emotional arguments break out in meetings where they are discussed. The pastor himself is trying to get everyone into the act of pondering the big question: why should we continue to run an organized Christian church on this corner of this community?

Why? Why, indeed? Isn't it assumed that Christians ought to go to church on Sunday and pay a pledge towards supporting it? Isn't our real problem simply lack of new members? Isn't that what we should be worried about: how do we find new members? How do we get our youth interested? How do we do attractive things that will bring people out to meetings and services? A hundred new members and our problems would be solved!

"The Lord is in His holy temple. Let all the earth keep silence before Him!" It is 11:00 A.M. on the dot and the service has begun in the suburbs. The beautifully robed thirty-voice choir marches with elegant dignity up the center aisle of the majestic nave as the congregation rises to sing the opening hymn of praise. More than three hundred people have come to this, the second service of the morning. The leader of worship gives the invocation, the Lord's Prayer is recited and all sit down. The choir sings, a Scripture lesson is read, a prayer is spoken and the offering is taken. Then, announcements are given.

"Be sure to remember that the ladies will meet on Tuesday for lunch and a program on overseas missions. The church board will meet Tuesday night for its monthly meet-

85

ing. The membership class will meet in the pastor's study on Saturday morning. Bible study group meets at the home of Mrs. Brown on Wednesday afternoon. Choir practices on Thursday evening and we urge anyone who likes to sing to come. The young people will meet tonight for a film on sexual morality. Any persons who wish to go to the Council of Churches annual dinner meeting are asked to make reservations with Mrs. Simpson before Friday noon. The clothing drive concludes in two weeks, so make sure you bring your donations and put them in the clothing barrel. Persons who desire to dedicate memorial flowers on Easter Sunday are asked to bring them to the church at least one hour before the service begins. Tickets for the pancake supper presented by the young people go on sale next week."

A hymn is sung, the sermon preached and the service concluded with a final hymn and benediction. The people appear to be friendly with each other, congenial to newcomers and most of them linger for some time at the coffee hour in the social hall. It has been a beautiful service, the choir has performed a magnificent anthem and the sermon has been most stimulating. The congregation is composed of young couples and families. They are proud of their new building, their smoothly running organizations and the good image that the congregation has in the eyes of the community. There is little conflict here, and the youth seem to take an interest in the programs devised for them.

The question of this parish's mission is not raised. It seems to have an idea of what it wants to do. It appears to have met the demands of its members, because its membership is on the upswing. It is a popular church and its leaders work well together.

At 11:00 A.M. in farming country, the pastor has just entered the front of the sanctuary during the organ prelude. He utters a call to worship and motions all to rise as he announces the opening hymn. The little building is filled with morning sun and about half full of worshipers. The service is informal. The pastor does not wear a robe, nor does the choir. A responsive reading is read by pastor and people, then the Lord's Prayer is repeated and then the *Gloria Patri* is sung. The people are then seated. The atmosphere is warm and cordial. The church building was built by the people themselves. A Scripture lesson is read and a prayer offered. A choir anthem is sung, another Scripture lesson read, and then a hymn. The announcements are then read to the people.

"Be sure to remember that the ladies will meet on Tuesday for lunch and a program on overseas missions. The church board will meet Tuesday night for its monthly meeting. The membership class will meet in the pastor's study on Saturday morning. Bible study group meets at the home of. . . ."

It is estimated that at least forty percent of the American population is in church every Sunday morning and an additional twenty percent are formally affiliated. Nevertheless, now, as never before in this century, the purpose of the local church is being hotly debated everywhere, not only in this country but literally everywhere.

It may not be as gross an exaggeration as it first sounds to suggest that most congregations are following the same basic form of activity. Though forms of morning worship differ vastly even within the same denomination, it is safe to claim that in most church people's minds, the Sunday worship service is the primary activity. And most of our services, even though we complain about them, seem to concentrate on the business of the parish. The announcements reveal the directions the organization is going, its values, its preoccupations.

When the word "mission" is heard in a typical congregation, certain rather specific images immediately come to the surface. Mission is considered to be a reference to work overseas, first of all. The church's mission usually is discussed as a process by which Christians here give money and supplies to send "over there," to help people less fortunate than ourselves. Missions speakers, missions programs, filmstrips, movies, printed promotional literature highlight, more often than not, the heroic work of a few Christians in foreign lands, working against great odds, taking healing and health to people who cannot help themselves. Eventually, we hear the proclamation that Christ is being taken to those people, that the gospel is being proclaimed in their midst. Stories are brought back through letters, articles and personal visits of mission speakers at mission dinners or mission festivals, about significant breakthroughs in the mission field.

A second familiar image that pops into our minds is mission as God's call to the congregation to which we belong. At least once a year, usually during the fall Every Member Canvass, and generally more often than that, we use phrases like "Our mission to our community," "God's work must truly be our own," "We are called to serve others in his name," etc. Into this context we attempt to make a case for all that we do in the church—that is, the material about which we make our Sunday morning announcements. What we really think we mean at that moment is: "Hear about the programs through which we are trying to carry out our mission to people in this community." In our church groups we plan many different programs which we genuinely hope will meet the needs of people. At year's end, we write up

88

reports about them all, give them at the annual meeting of the congregation and call that a report of our year's advance in mission. Sometimes we say that we are building the kingdom of God as we increase attendance.

A third popular image of mission is the very personal one. When we are not speaking about the programs of our congregation, we are probably speaking about our personal commitment to the Christian faith, our spiritual life and our commitment to do God's will. Personal devotions are encouraged and personal behavior is emphasized as the principal way by which Christians bring about changes in the lives of others around them in the outside world. One's own sense of mission is a highly emotional topic sometimes, and we use effective music and poetic language in our worship services and summer camps to give people a sense of God's nearness. Quite often a congregation's morning worship service concludes with a "hymn of dedication" or an "act of commitment," and the order of service will display such a slogan as "Enter to pray; depart to serve."

By these three categories, at least, we usually wrap up the word "mission" neatly and live with it comfortably. It goes without saying that humans are imperfect and can never completely fulfill the missions to which they think they are called. Therefore, we will just do our best and a forgiving God will give us strength. Or so the story goes.

But there is ferment in the ranks. Young people—and older people who think freshly—are quarreling with the given premises of churches where they live. Intellectually, they are attacking beliefs. Emotionally, they are simply pulling out. A new period of debate and dialogue is giving birth to "underground" movements of those who stay in the church but now seek to work radical changes in it. And it all has to do with mission.

The whole world is before us now, the whole family of man, the totality of human interrelationships and responsibilities. The planetary man has become a reality. And those who view human existence in a more completely human way are voicing and acting out their disaffection with all institutions—government, schools and churches—that are oriented around ingrown, parochial, small minded concerns and activities. How can people who call themselves Christians, these people are asking, sit in a beautiful building once a week and repeat other-worldly clichés and platitudes that shut them off from Vietnam, the rising revolutions in Africa and Latin America, the over forty million people on the American continent who live in poverty, the pressing problems which face teeming masses in cities and the struggles of minorities for their share of justice, power and freedom?

A student has put his rebellion into words in an open letter to the adults of his denomination:

You don't let us vote or drink. We are governed by people of your choice. We fight in the wars you make—and die to keep you free. We are still expected to do so quietly, without trying to change anything.

You choose our college. You loan or withhold the car. You co-sign our bankbooks. You instill as many of your prejudices and inhibitions and neuroses into us as you can; and then constantly expect us to explode like a time bomb. You choose our clothes, criticize our friends, deprecate our books, our music, our heroes and our ideals.

You mistrusted your parents for giving you the Depression and the War and Victorian Morality, but we didn't live through those things. You have experienced such climactic events that Vietnam is a brushfire war to you. But to us such a thing is a major calamity—especially with your draft.

You do not for a minute think that we might govern ourselves decently; and this insult to our intelligence—and to all of your training, too—is what makes us so eager to rebel. We don't like your society or your government or your morality or your philosophy or your religion or your tradition!

You think we're Quixotes, but we're out to make our own New World. We've had enough of yours. And if you get in our way, watch out!

We're not all beatniks or Vietniks, but we're mostly all rebels. We don't consider ourselves reformers. We are a grim generation, grimly rolling up its sleeves, grimly setting to work, grimly getting the job done. We're already tired, rather than exuberant.

You sent your missionaries; we send ourselves. You spoke of democracy around the world; we speak of democracy across the street. You isolated; we reach.

Our high school diplomas mean more education than Bachelor's Degrees once meant. We know more about religion than Paul, more about physics than Newton, more about chemistry than Boyle or Lavoisier, more about biology than Darwin, more about sociology than Marx, more about politics than Jefferson, more about philisophy than Plato, more about geography than Mercator, more about history than Macaulay.

We are unashamedly proud of our intellects. We cannot be conservative if that means sacrificing human liberty and dignity to Big Brother. We cannot be moderate if that means being spineless and undecided. We have our morality; we have our politics; we have our social schema. Educate us, then leave us alone and we shall do the same.

Sociologists have been describing the breakdown in the family as a social unit. Do you think that after years of education and counseling and investigation that we are not more ready for the world than you were? Or are? Then you delude yourself. We have been trained for the world—and now you would attempt to deny it to us? Watch out!

This young student might be called brash, to put it mildly—arrogant, proud and, perhaps, dangerous. But whatever might be said of him negatively, his sentiments do not shock anyone today who knows what is going on in the world. His point of view is that of a growing number of youth and adults. His prophecy is a prophecy of a new era in human history. He is, after all, rather accurate about what the new world looks like. And his statement is, in the most profound sense, a statement about mission. His passion is for new, relevant, human mission, involvements that release human beings from the scourges of war, disease, hunger and ignorance so that they might truly belong to a race of fully human humans.

His words, we must remember, sound very much like those in the book of Jeremiah which describe that young prophet's vision about himself and his world.

Then I said, "Ah, Lord God! Behold, I do not know how to speak, for I am only a youth." But the Lord said to me, "Do not say, 'I am only a youth';
for to all to whom I send you you shall go,
and whatever I command you you shall speak.
Be not afraid of them,
for I am with you to deliver you. . . .
Behold, I have put my words in your mouth.
See, I have set you this day over nations and over kingdoms,
to pluck up and to break down,
to destroy and to overthrow,
to build and to plant." (Jeremiah 1:6-10)

Jesus made many similar prophetic utterances. On the famous Palm Sunday entry into Jerusalem, for example, a momentary blast occurred that we usually ignore in our branch-waving worship services.

And when he drew near and saw the city he wept over it, saying, "Would that even today you knew the things that make for peace! But now they are hid from your eyes. For the days shall come upon you, when your enemies will cast up a bank about you and surround you, and hem you in on every side, and dash you to the ground, you and your children within you, and they will not leave one stone upon another in you; because you did not know the time of your visitation." (Luke 19:41-44)

Christians tend to believe that life in the church is supposed to be nice. It never has been correctly understood that way, but the malady lingers on, the illusion of safety and purity is perpetuated. The student has seen properly through that, because he is interested in mission. A church without radical involvement in the world's agonies and turmoils is a church without mission, no matter how many millions of people it involves in church-type activities. And a church without mission is hardly a church at all. Diane E. Mann writes:

> 'I built a church'
> There were no walls
>   no one is outside
> The pews were lined in green
>   or they were foxholes
> I think
> 'I built a church'
> Ordained a god and priested a man
>   and his vestments were gold and rags
> 'I built a church'
> With rocks and straw
>   and slaves' sweat
>   and sweated contributions
> 'But I built a church'

The choir was a million voices
  but no one sang
The altar faced to the East, and West
  and up and down
The chalice was made of tin
  and rusted
And the wafers were green
'But I built a church'
And the church stood for a million years
The priest died
The altar rotted
Then a storm came up and washed away my church
In the cool of a gothic setting
  spires high—awe besetting
Men kneel at the brass rail
  icons stare
  convictions fail
At the baptismal font
  water purges
  sin not want
In the shadow of the tree
  lurkes the image
  one or three[2]

8 The New Scene

We are in a new epoch, and we face a new church situation and a new mission. But how do we use the word "new"? Do we mean new to us, new for our experience, new in the sense that we've never been here before? Do we mean *new* in the overall sense, in what might be called the eternal, biblical sense? In Isaiah it is written, "Behold, I am doing a new thing; it springs forth, do you not perceive it?" (43:19) Yet in Ecclesiastes we find, "What has been is what will be, and what has been done is what will be done; and there is nothing new under the sun. Is there a thing of which it is said, 'See, this is new'? It has been already, in the ages before us." (1:9-10) Revelation contains the marvelous words: "Then I saw a new heaven and a new earth; for the first heaven and the first earth had passed away. . . . And he who sat upon the throne said, 'Behold, I make all things new.'" (21:1, 5)

Jesus spoke in terms of newness all the time. One of the best known of his sayings is about the wineskins: "No one sews a piece of unshrunk cloth on an old garment; if he does, the patch tears away from it, the new from the old, and a worse tear is made. And no one puts new wine into old wineskins; if he does, the wine will burst the skins, and the wine is lost, and so are the skins; but new wine is for fresh skins." (Mk. 2:21-22)

But despite the public clamor ("What is this? A new teaching!"), and even despite his own insistence upon a break with the hold of the past, Jesus kept pointing out how he was a son of the Jewish household of faith and a product of the law and the prophets. All his thoughts and motivations sprang directly out of his roots in the tradition. He was a revolutionary because of his contemporary radical applications of the biblical heritage; he was a conservative because of his identification with values that had been maintained through hundreds of generations before him. "Therefore every scribe who has been trained for the kingdom of heaven is like a householder who brings out of his treasure what is new and what is old." (Matt. 13:52) It's not either/or; it's both/and.

When we speak of "new" forms of mission, therefore, we keep in mind that our roots are with the heritage out of which we have come as humans and Christians. In that sense, Ecclesiastes is correct; "there is nothing new under the sun." The human story and the search for justice are not very new at all.

But in the sense of our time in history, everything is absolutely new in possibility and promise. This moment is born in a kind of freedom from all other moments. It has never happened before and we do not necessarily have to treat it according to tried and true formulae. We always stand at an intersection of the past and the future, and our decisions determine the location of the next intersection, and so it goes. Another word for it is destiny. We do not believe in blind fate that is predestined or ordained somewhere else. Rather, we live out our hopes, drives and commitments and create new destinies as a result.

How do we proceed in the new time we see upon us? Three basic questions must be asked every time we hear ourselves talking about a new activity that we say advances or fulfills the mission of the church. These questions are interrelated. They must be asked as one question.

First, *are we committed to the radical search for facts?* "Facts" sounds terribly scientific. It means "the whole truth and nothing but the truth," that is, a continual probing into the reality of the persons, places and situations involved. If we are gearing up for a project in our neighborhood, it means trying to know all of the elements in that neighborhood. It may mean scientific surveys that bring statistical data about a community's needs. But it also may mean prophetic probings through other means—artistic events, public meetings of protest, informal conversation with people. A commitment to the radical search for facts is a commitment to a never ending openness to the news of the real situations in which we find ourselves.

No advance into the world can be made by a church that is filled with magnificent intentions but is really uninformed. Eugene O'Neill's play, *The Hairy Ape,* provides the most eloquent statement of this imperative. He depicts the religious social worker who desperately wants to do good deeds for the "unfortunate" men who shovel coal in the holds of steamships. But she has no idea of their situation, and when she finally meets one in person the confrontation is both hilarious and tragic.

When a small parish in the Midwest decided to initiate a new form of ministry for the town's young people, it gathered youth and adults of the church together for meetings and quickly set up a new structure. All the right ideas and best motives were basic to the organization. It stumbled immediately, however, when the nonchurch persons in the town displayed either no interest or scorn for the project. After a few weeks of reflection, the church group abandoned their original approach and chose a slower process of fact-finding and cooperation with other groups outside the church.

This leads to our second question: *are we committed to the ecumenical search for wholeness?* Constantinos Doxiadis is a Greek architect and urban planner. Although his home and main office are in Athens, his firm reaches around the world. Mr. Doxiadis's name has often been before us in recent years as he has articulated the challenges which confront the human race within the next century in terms of his living environments. When world population reaches thirty billion, says he, man will actually be living in a universal city which covers the entire planet, an "ecumenopolis." He calls for people now to lay good foundations for that not too distant time.

"I think we have a twofold obligation," he explains. "First, to study man as a whole, without rejecting anything that he has learned throughout his history unless we can prove scientifically that it is harmful. This we can achieve not by coordinating existing sciences—man does not consist of externally coordinated parts, since he forms a whole—but by Anthropics, the Science of Man. Second, in the absence of any proof that we can produce a better man by changing the relationship between the body, the sense, the mind, and the soul, we should work toward a complete man with a harmonious development of all his elements, a total man whom I cannot name anything but *human man.*" [1]

The word "ecumenical" that Dr. Doxiadis uses comes from a Greek word meaning "household." We have heard it recently used in reference to that movement in which Christians are growing closer together. Ecumenism, the movement toward completeness in the "household," refers to two kinds of unity among Christians. On the one hand, by virtue of our Christian identity we already have unity through the single force of Jesus Christ, the key figure who draws all of us into acts of response, love and hope.

This kind of unity is manifest through those activities in which Christians of all communions cooperate in mutual and common ministries. Councils of churches, local and national, bring workers of Protestant, Orthodox, and, increasingly, Roman Catholic bodies into a unity of ministry. The World Council of Churches, with offices in Geneva, Switzerland, not only joins Protestant and Orthodox Christians of every land, but it is now in communication with the offices of the Vatican.

We have entered a new era of trusting among Christians. It is even now possible for us to say, "one on behalf of all." If one denomination or congregation is performing a ministry, then it is done on my behalf, even though I belong to another family of church identity. There is no need for me to duplicate it. In this new time, it is possible for me simply to recognize it as representing me and to support it in all ways possible.

On the other hand, a more organic unity is now emerging as a possibility among some Christians. This pertains to the actual joining together of ecclesiastical bodies. The United Church of Christ in the United States, for instance, is the product of a merger between the Evangelical and Reformed Church and the Congregational Christian Churches. The United Presbyterian Church in the U.S.A. is the result of the union of the United Presbyterian Church with the Presbyterian Church in the U.S.A. The Methodist Church and the Evangelical United Brethren Church consummated a merger in the spring of 1968. The United Church of Canada came about over 40 years ago as a merger of several churches. The Anglican Church of Canada and the United Church are now discussing possibilities of their uniting.

The Consultation on Church Union represents the very ambitious desire of ten American denominations to do two things: first, to explore the unity which they know they have already; second, to agree upon the basis of actual union which might bring them all into one corporate church body in the future. The members of the COCU are: African Methodist Episcopal, African Methodist Episcopal Zion, Christian Methodist Episcopal, Disciples of Christ (Christian Churches), Episcopal, Evangelical United Brethren, Methodist, Presbyterian Church in the U.S., United Church of Christ, United Presbyterian Church in the U.S.A. Several other denominations are participant-observers to this process. COCU represents a beginning in the painful, slow process of re-finding one another through walls of scriptural, doctrinal, theological interpretations of the church's faith and practice, and then acting in oneness.

But Dr. Doxiadis would remind us that Christians do not own the word "ecumenism." Outside of the Christian family exists the family of mankind, only a minority of whom are

Christians. The business at hand, he would assert, is to find a style of life in the world which is truly ecumenical in the secular sense, ecumenical in that it concentrates on all structures, all groups, all barriers, all identities, all cultures that either prevent man or assist man in the imperative struggle toward becoming "human man" in the total, planetary culture that is now emerging as never before.

"Secular ecumenicity" refers to our acknowledging our belonging to a variety of movements. It means that even government agencies belong to *the mission*. Civil liberties groups, for example, defend the rights of all men when they decide to fight for the civil rights of Nazis or any persecuted group. La Huelga, the striking farm workers in the southwestern United States, act out a mission on behalf of all migrant workers when they press for the bargaining powers as a labor union to negotiate for better wages and working conditions. It means that channels of reconciliation must be found, however painful and difficult may be the process, between the conflicting French and English heritage groups of Canada, in order that the human worth and dignity and the rich cultural contributions of all be preserved and enhanced. Ecumenical planners are committed to a secular concept of ecumenism. No force is insignificant; every association of people belongs to the whole network that groans in travail as a new era of human possibility is born.

The major test before any project or program undertaken by a church or group of churches is the test for its true ecumenical nature. We can no longer justify institution building simply because we have money and people. We can no longer justify denominational or congregational preoccupations simply because things are going well and people are clamoring for more growth. We can no longer justify even the money we put out for salaries of clergy and other

101

personnel simply because we like their work. All of this must add up to something new, because the world is one and it is in anything but perfect shape. All of this must integrate into the stream of human upbuilding on the human scale to make the world society a human phenomenon and not a bleak, technologically sterile one. In short, the church is called into the fray of ecumenical mission on all levels—the struggle to manifest our unity in the Spirit, the struggle to find real corporate unity among Christians and the struggle to face the gigantic issues that now confront humanity.

In "local" terms, this means that interesting choices must be made. Which is more truly missionary, in the sense described above: a dinner to raise money to buy school books for Latin American, church-supported schools, or a meeting of an action committee for improving the schools in a depressed area of our own city? It may be unfair to pose this kind of question, but the usual congregation thinks that the first choice sounds more "missionary." It is also easier to do and is less controversial. It brings certain feelings of satisfaction to one who contributes, especially if a "missionary" filmstrip report comes from Latin America with visual evidence of how far the good deed has gone among people less fortunate than the giver. The need is pressing and obviously legitimate.

But the school committee is no less so. Only, it is far more questionable and the issues less clear cut. Resistance to accepting involvement in this form of mission is great among church people. But is the need less noble, the cause less glaring, than Latin American situations? Rather than make qualitative judgment between the two, can we not reckon them a part of the same mission? If one gives money to send overseas, should not one be ready for risky engagements with identical issues in one's own neighborhood?

In a western region, where fair housing ordinances have been the subject of fiery public debates, congregations, pastors, lay people and denominational leaders declared themselves in favor of open housing without regard to race, color, creed or religion. Since that time financial support of the churches has been withdrawn by great numbers of church people. Matters got worse when church identification with the striking grapepickers was publicized. And for others, the straw to break the camel's back was the new ministry among "social misfits." Many of those who pulled out their money announced that they were donating more to "foreign missions." Could they really believe that their response was now a more faithful one? Surely they did not comprehend the real situation abroad, where such a phrase as "foreign missions" is now looked upon with contempt bordering on hatred. Condescension and paternalism by North Americans continue to live side by side with self-righteous support of programs designed to advance the American Way of Life among the people of the world, but they are called "missions" programs. In reality, the scathing, ecumenical nature of mission aches to be included on the agendas of the churches.

And now we have anticipated the third question: *are we committed to the risk involved?* We can become pretty paranoid about this kind of question. Church publications have reproduced some terribly sentimental accounts of so-called risk, which have been in very poor taste. "Dr. and Mrs. X actually went four years without a hi-fi set or television, so dedicated were they to the unfortunate people of Angola." Or: "Tim Smith, a lawyer, has given up all of his nights at home so that he could run a coffeehouse for the deprived youth of the southeast sector of the city." We can glorify sacrifices until they are objects of intense pride. We can arrive at a point where we feel uncomfortable unless we are suffering and can take satisfaction in how we are denying ourselves the things we really would like to have. This is inverse (or perverse) navel-gazing.

The true risk of mission lies elsewhere. It does not have to do with the risks that come from doing good deeds that people can observe; rather, the risks to the self, the inner predicament of changing one's idea of who one is and what one wants in life. A moving illustration of the poignant, internal challenge occurred recently in Abington Township, Pennsylvania, a comfortable suburb north of Philadelphia. Dr. Allan Glatthorn, the principal of the high school, is a Quaker with strong feelings about peace and brotherhood. He has never tried to hide his ideas about the role of religious people in society, but he has concentrated primarily on his administrative office and has succeeded in building up a program of variety, sensitivity and recognized educational excellence for the school district.

As United States involvement in southeast Asia reached more violent proportions, Dr. Glatthorn was torn with agony over the bloodshed and the large issues that the war in Vietnam has raised before the entire nation. He therefore participated in a silent peace vigil on a street in his town one weekend.

The reactions of people in the community were mixed, but enough were hostile to his behavior that the board of education was forced to hold a debate on the issue: should a high school principal, who is a public official, make a public display of his opposition to the policy of the nation? The crisis eventually subsided after considerable support was voiced in favor of Dr. Glatthorn's right to behave as he chose as a private citizen. In the midst of that controversy, Dr. Glatthorn decided to speak directly to his students about

104

himself, and the substance of his communication reveals the stature of one man who knows the risk of mission. In an open letter published in the school newspaper he wrote:

Last summer I grew a beard but shaved it off when asked, even though I liked it. Last month I took part in a silent protest about an issue of national importance, and acted independently, even though there was much public criticism.

And ever since some students and parents have asked some important questions: Why did I grow a beard? Why did I shave it off? Why did I protest? What right do I have to take a stand on a matter of public controversy?

So maybe it's time to answer as honestly as I can and to talk about the lessons that are involved in both situations.

I grew a beard because it's harmless fun to play with the externals—the way we look and the way we dress. And I grew a beard to suggest that you can't judge a man by appearances. I'm the same man without a beard as I was with one. And, in the same way, you can't judge a student by long hair or short skirts. And maybe I grew a beard to show that we do have some small personal rights which we should value. I hope that you cherish your right to be yourself both in the little ways of dress and clothing and in the big issues of peace and war and brotherhood and justice.

But I shaved off the beard because I was asked to do so, and because my desire to express a little bit of my individuality had become a major problem for others, and because people were seeing the beard, not the man behind the beard. A man has to choose the battles he will fight, and he has to weigh the consequences of his actions against the importance of the issue. . . . So beard on, beard off—a little issue that wasn't worth a fight. But what of the other protest?

I stood silently on a street corner in Jenkintown because of my love for my country, and my belief in my religion; I stood there as a parent, as a citizen, and as a principal. I don't want you to think about my views on Vietnam—I won't even discuss them—but I do want you to think of the meaning of my actions. And maybe there are these lessons:

First, there's a war going on, with lives and issues and your future at stake. And it's more important than dates and cars and hairstyles and beards. In four or five years you and your friends might be in that war, and you had better find out for yourself what it's all about.

Second, there is a lesson about patriotism. Patriotism is love of country, and love of country, at its best, will sometimes combine open criticism with loyal support. All love—of country, of family, of school—includes criticism. I love my children, but discipline them; I love my school, but complain about its faults; I love my country but will protest when I think it is wrong.

But criticism doesn't mean subversion. I discipline my children but will protect them from harm. I will criticize my country but support it in every way that I can. And I hope that in the major issues of your life you can combine honest difference with loyal support.

There's a third lesson about conformity and rebellion. Most students conform and a few rebel—but there's a middle ground between conformity and rebellion. If you always believe what you are told and always do what the mass of people expect, you surrender your individuality. But on the other hand, if you rebel and break the law, you begin to destroy the law, the very thing that holds society together and protects your basic rights. For me, the middle ground is responsible legal protest that does not infringe on the rights of others. . . .

And there's a lesson about the need for courage. A man must stand up for the important things he believes in. The problems we face as a nation—war, communism, discrimination, poverty—will be solved only by those who have the courage to stand up and be counted. I respect those individuals who differ openly with me on this particular issue because they too are standing up in protest, and in a democracy, healthy constructive debate will produce better answers than any single voice that claims to know the truth. I hope that you too will stand up and be counted for the big things you believe in. Your school and your country will be the better for it.

And there's an important lesson about the consequences of courage. Every protest you make will involve you and all those around you in serious consequences. And you had better be sure that the issue is important enough to run the risks that protest always brings. I am not alone. What I do affects my family, my school, my community, and my country. And always I have to weigh the gains made against the damage done.

And that is where I am now. I can take the angry criticism and the bad publicity and the anonymous letters. But if my family is hurt, or if my school is injured, or if my community is torn asunder by controversy, or if in some way my country is damaged, then I will still my voice and pray the wounds will heal.

I want to close on a personal note about you and me. I don't want to be a rebel. I love peace and order too much to seek rebellion. I don't think that I'm a hero. I know my weaknesses and faults too well for that.

But I will try to be a man. And that is all that I ask of you. When the issues are important, try to act with wisdom and with courage, and with love. You may make mistakes. You may get hurt. Others may dislike you. But if you act the man, you keep your self-respect and those around you are somehow the better for it.

And maybe in the long run that's what school is all about—to help you find your own way to manhood. God be with you as you struggle.

The impression made by Dr. Glatthorn upon his students was mixed. Many did not agree with his viewpoint but supported his right to act it out in the open as a citizen. One boy wrote in the school paper: "The cause Dr. Glatthorn is supporting is an unpopular one. It is this fact, however, that should make his actions particularly worthy in the eyes of parents raising children who will become the good, patriotic citizens of tomorrow. Regardless of one's opinion of the cause being pursued, all members of our community should be proud of the actions of Dr. Glatthorn, a man who has the courage of his convictions."

Other students flatly refused him the right to protest. One letter to the editor said, "Doesn't he realize that his gallant but unnecessary stand, though important to him as an educator and a man, might result in the ruination of all that he and the rest of the faculty and student body have worked so hard to attain? It is my opinion that Dr. Glatthorn should sacrifice his stand in order to preserve his program."

Dr. Glatthorn has always favored controversy as a basic experience for growth and maturity. Abington Township was embroiled in it for several weeks. He had come to the point where some form of action had to be taken. He had surmised the risk. He had acted. He had been ready for the price to be paid. He paid it.

We have no way of knowing just what the results of Dr. Glatthorn's actions have been in the lives of all persons around him, near and far. But the point is that we do not have to know. Indeed, it is not important that we should know. Results that are quickly understood have never been at the heart of the church's mission. The ancient image of missionaries winning thousands to Christianity must be totally shattered. All that we do know, and it brings considerable power and hope to know this, is that a man did a thing in which he believed with love and courage. That is all we really need to know.

To achieve in ourselves what Myron Bloy calls a "tolerance for ambiguity" is a most difficult stumbling block for contemporary Christians, and any true mission depends upon our facing into, not sidestepping, this difficulty. Our only real possession is hope. Our hope is in the power of the force that has brought us into life and which renews life. We call this force God. Our hope is in the potential hidden in the creation, that continues to pulse on into new forms of hopefulness. Our knowledge of all this is focused by our comprehension of a concrete activity which happens among men—Christ. But after we have made these theological reflections, we must confront a maze of complex situations. Armed with hope we plunge into them. We easily get our noses bloodied, but we often break through into fantastic new levels of existence. And so our hope is renewed and we step farther, more boldly. But the ambiguity of the world never disappears, nor will it conform to our efforts to simplify it. In other words, to be a Christian is to take the fantastic risk that one can be totally wrong about everything. And that is a really real risk to the old ego.

We recognize how fear is the basis of hostility against things we don't fully understand. The stubborn conservatism that fights until the last drop of blood against progress in a congregation or a city council or a state legislature or a school club usually stems from fright in the face of the unfamiliar. That fear is supposedly wiped out by hope in the experience of a Christian, or at least almost wiped out. The freedom to put oneself in the position of failure is the real freedom which Jesus kept talking about and his disciples struggled to understand. "Perfect love casts out fear," said John, and that is where it's at for a contemporary Christian, that kind of release, liberty from the drag of faintheartedness. People like Dr. Glatthorn walk into their confrontations with concrete scenes of conflict without absolute certainties as to the outcome or even their own wisdom, but they do have a quiet courage of the spirit. It is a Martin

Luther-type action: "Here I stand. I can do no other. God help me!" This is a fabulous saying.

Mission, then, is built upon a kind of audacity. The church has participated in new, vigorous missionary service on behalf of the world only when individuals finally "felt religion" about an issue and literally performed a *breakout*.

> *I wait. Every day I minister*
> *to the tattered faces of the wounded, fresh*
> *from their lunatic and haggard wars;*
> *they don't return with me,*
> *but I take the risk for their sake*
> *and because I have been slandered*
> *by a stranger. I'll never find out*
> *whether what I'm doing is right, friend,*
> *and neither will you. . . .*
> *Someone will meet me,*
> *but there's no need of that now.*
> *Is it time? I stand where we are: scavengers,*
> *glowing like dead bark, glide and clash*
> *in the alleys, assassins scuffle for the knife,*
> *but I stand where we are. Summer*
> *is full-blooded, preening for the harvest moon.*
> *I'm never certain when the time is ripe!*
> *If I consume everything, now,*
> *Will the banquet prove my suspicion?*
> *Bubbling to my hilarious tongue*
> *a million accidents of flesh explode:*
> *I can't be empty! A laugh in the face!*
> *I'll aim at sunset with the old grim joy.*
> *Something always being born, blotting out the womb.*[2]

9 Renewal and Breakout

A full-page advertisement appeared in *The Plain Dealer* of Cleveland, Ohio, the day before Thanksgiving, 1966. Pictured was a can of dog food on a table next to a lighted candle.

"Thanksgiving special: 17¢ a pound," the ad announced. "If you're on public welfare in Cleveland you can serve each child with one of these swell dinners and have enough left over for seconds. Because every family on public assistance is entitled to 73¢ a day for each child. Even on Thanksgiving day. And Christmas. 73¢ a day to bring up a child. Feed him. Clothe him. Buy him books. And this is shocking. Because Cleveland is in the fourth wealthiest state in property. Fifth in personal income. Third in manufacturing. But 30th in aid to needy families with children. That's right. 30th. All year 'round. Thanksgiving and Christmas included. You can hardly spend much less than that. And it shows. For Thanksgiving this year, don't just deliver a basket of food to the poor. Write and ask the governor to raise public assistance to a realistic minimum standard. 40,520 Cleveland kids shouldn't have to think that holidays are more days of doing without. The address is Governor Rhodes, State House, Columbus, Ohio. Don't wait. Do it today. Council of Churches of Christ of Greater Cleveland." [1]

This "publishing event" can be called a *breakout*. In the experience of the "swinging" people in the region at the time, it was "way out," a radical—surprisingly radical—form of witness for the church to make. Here were some Christian missionaries intent on doing a job, and not terribly anxious about swelling the ranks of their congregations— graceful people with no strings attached to their idea of mission. They put a message to the entire population of a city in a forceful way, announcing, in effect, that we of the church want you to know that this is where Christianity belongs, mixed up in the controversies, confronting the powers and principalities that govern human beings and regulate the environments where human beings work and live.

To remain healthy, one must question institutionalized forms of Christianity. This is our only safeguard against idolatry in a time which tends to idolize institutions. We have become a society of corporations—financial, merchandising, governmental, cultural, social and religious corporations. It is not naturally human to worship corporations. It is more naturally human to find one's identity elsewhere. Therefore, I am pessimistic about all institutionalized patterns of existence, for they try to squeeze me into molds of all kinds even when I do not give my consent to be manipulated and squeezed.

The institutional church is in trouble today. Denominations are complaining about the loss of grass roots support. Local parishes are hysterical about the loss of youth and young, sophisticated members. For the first time in several decades church affiliation is slipping behind the annual population increase. Experts are asked with greater urgency, "How can we develop *more effective* programs to make the church more relevant?" This question usually means, "How can we make the church more popular, attractive, sought after by modern man?"

One reason for the institutional church's trouble is its failure to keep its thinking fresh. Theologically, many of our words, worship services, thought patterns and basic assumptions are almost identical to what they were before World War I and earlier. Contemporary man, inhabiting an empirical age, born into an era of reason, logic and scientific process, will not stand for metaphysical mumbo jumbo. Clergy and seminaries have not exerted the maximum effort to push theological reflection to the frontier, where it can engage in the discussions of technologists, social scientists, politicians, scientists and the other specialists of our epoch.

Another reason for the institutional church's trouble is its failure to act in the arena where the great issues of the human race are determined. Churches have rarely taken initiative in acting on behalf of humanity. They have almost always followed someone else's lead. This has lost for them the respect of sophisticated and oppressed peoples alike.

But during recent years, in all religious bodies, two kinds of movements have been gathering force. A "renewal" move-

113

ment has become obvious, a great pooling of resources and knowledge for the refurbishing of the institutional church so that it can become more flexible for missionary activity. The other movement has developed almost like an epidemic; we may call it the breakout. This is a movement in which Christians are leaving traditional church structures and finding or creating new ones designed for a specific piece of work.

The "renewal" movement is important, but it has failed, so far, to challenge the traditional institutional church very deeply. Committees, boards, proposals, studies, research and discussions can become traps for good ideas. By the time some persons on the official board have been talked into approving a creative project, the time of ripeness has passed.

When James Meredith tried to enter the University of Mississippi as the first Afro-American student, several days of violence exploded. Before it was over two newspaper reporters had been shot to death on the lawn of the university and scores of persons injured by bullets, clubs, tear gas and bricks. During the night of the most heated armed battle, a parish board was meeting within four blocks of the action to discuss the details of the new sprinkler system they had decided to install. It was considered to be one of the more liberal churches in Oxford, Mississippi.

And reflective people wonder what preoccupies church boards in a city such as Dearborn, Michigan, the automobile center of the hemisphere, while nearby Detroit burns and the U.S.-Canadian border has to be regulated during a time of "racial violence."

The "renewal" movement works slowly in a time of rapid change, change that comes at a computer pace, change that bombards us from all sides with new information, new necessities. Some churches, we should be ready to admit, should close their doors. Can we say that God wills for a congregation to spend money on its building and its minister while it remains intact as a small interest group desirous of retreating from the world? The "renewal" movement fails when it assumes that God intends for us to nurse churches back to health by new means, new programs, new efforts to get people interested in our churches. A church that finally closes its doors has not been canceled out. It has served its purpose. Now, however, the mission of the church may be centered elsewhere.

Breakout is taking place among students. The Student Nonviolent Coordinating Committee and the Students for a Democratic Society, to name two different organizations, are pressure groups built by students. These groups have had profound effects on our culture. They have revolted against social norms, they have led demonstrations and extreme behavior such as draft card burning. We may not comprehend what they mean by all of this. We must try. In spite of whatever emotional reactions we have to someone like Stokely Carmichael, it should be obvious to us that these loosely formed associations of active students perform an invaluable service. They inform, challenge, focus and exert pressure on behalf of the ideals that all of us say we support.

The S.D.S. is linked to the Radical Education Project, a serious effort to break through the problem of education's isolation from the real world of pressure and rapid change. These workers are doing research in community power centers. They maintain research projects in several cities and support the activities of community organizers among minority groups who are trying to break into a public education system that doesn't seem to know their problems.

115

Ramparts magazine is another example of a *breakout* away from traditional church renewal ideas. Founded by Roman Catholic laymen, it now considers itself simply radical. It has begun to win awards for journalistic excellence. It shrinks from no task in its muckraking. Its campaigns against secret activities in government—such as the C.I.A.—and the military-industrial complex that promotes war—have gotten it more enemies than friends, although at last report *Ramparts* was circulating more widely than *Harper's* and *Atlantic* magazines combined. And yet *Ramparts* has expressed in one of its circulars its purpose for going into newsstand, slick magazine competition with these words: "to revitalize the Judeo-Christian ethic; to insure the dignity of all men by eradicating war, racism, poverty and other evils that degrade the human spirit; to break down the walls that divide men, and build up the things that unite them—the raw force of true artistic creativity, the sublime idea that can raise the mind and unfreeze the heart."

In the arts, Judson Memorial Church in Greenwich Village, New York, has led the church away from old concepts of "religious drama" into totally new realms of theater. In fact, the work, at the Judson Poet's Theater, of Al Carmines and Larry Kornfeld has attracted devotion and respect from the cultural establishment of New York City. In Toronto, Montreal, Minneapolis and San Francisco similar efforts in dance, music and drama, which often appear to be anti-art in their weird abstract absurdity, are giving birth to a new era of art as total involvement.

One day a group of Roman Catholic laymen appeared at a public hearing of a housing authority in a large city. The issue was *de facto* racial segregation in two of the units. The churchmen were there to testify in favor of building new units of public housing on sites far away from the Negro ghetto, so that a measure of integration would begin to be achieved. When they were asked by a television reporter why they were there, one of them, a respected elementary school teacher, said, "Jesus wants it." That may appear to be a rude, overly simplified, even dangerously superficial answer. Coming from this man, however, it meant a *breakout* phrase in that situation.

"In view of the revolutionary age in which we live, celebrate and plot," writes Paul Kittlaus in a church newsletter, "attempts to design any neat systems of thought and feeling response are not likely to be finalized. The question raised is whether our gathering develops in our people a capacity to handle, reflect upon and act within this revolutionary and ambiguous world? In other words, does the gathering of the community aid in the process of creating free and involved persons; do strategies develop, giving the members of the community some sense of how they are to make their contributions of thought and action within the larger framework of God's people at work in the world.

"Are we facing directly and without evasion the reality of the dying of the old age and the birth of the new, and are we participating therein? Are we taking upon ourselves both the joy and the agony of our time and of each other in such a way as to put us in touch with depth rather than superficial life processes and resources of forgiveness and love and of prophetic anger? Are we enabled by our series of gathering of the community-in-mission to enter into our individual life tasks with new resources of hope, which means both concern for justice and of love; and are we empowered to stretch beyond the narrow confines which we tend to build around ourselves and to enter into increasingly larger visions of life's call to responsibility?"

117

Those of us over twenty-five hear ourselves cautioning youthful impatience with: "Discretion is the better part of valor," or something like that. But another cliché seems to be every bit as biblical and more to the point: "Fools rush in where angels fear to tread." Paul said that he was a "fool for Christ," and this age certainly appears to demand a foolishness such as that of the great New Testament missionary. And so we dare to welcome the progressions through "renewal" to *breakout* and we dare to encourage the wildest forms of experimentation in missionary activity. Mission can assume nearly any form, so long as it is approached with a radical search for the full truth of an issue, is founded on an ecumenical wholeness, involves theological reflection and entails real risk for oneself. Hear Dylan Thomas in "Our Eunuch Dreams" IV:

> *This is the world: the lying likeness of*
> *Our strips of stuff that tatter as we move*
> *Loving and being loath;*
> *The dream that kicks the buried from their sack*
> *And lets their trash be honoured as the quick.*
> *This is the world. Have faith.*
>
> *For we shall be a shouter like the cock,*
> *Blowing the old dead back; our shots shall smack*
> *The image from the plates;*
> *And we shall be fit fellows for a life,*
> *And who remain shall flower as they love,*
> *Praise to our faring hearts.*[2]

10 Mission Impossible

Go therefore and make disciples of all nations, baptizing them in the name of the Father and of the Son and of the Holy Spirit, teaching them to observe all that I have commanded you; and lo, I am with you always, to the close of the age." Matthew 28:19-20

Is this a square way to open a chapter? You bet it is! At first glance it may smack of regression back to those "wornout phrases" away from *breakout*. Or, it might sound like a sell-out. "Ah, here comes the pitch, just like Sunday school." Actually, it is neither. The Great Commission quoted above stands as a part of our heritage, a key part, in that it has been cited as one of the great texts motivating the expansion of the church throughout the world during the past nineteen centuries. The exploration and settling of European territory and the New World took place under its banner, and the development of education, health and literacy in large regions of Africa and Asia has risen directly as a result of its imperative. Historically, it is central to any person's comprehension of the civilization of Western man and, in large measure, of world history since the time of Christ.

To be sure, from our vantage point and with hindsight we can make judgments about injustices and gross errors committed by those missionaries whose interpretation of those two verses led them to believe that they had to coerce the whole world into giving outward obedience to the Christian church. That, too, is a part of history now, and we are children, heirs of that history. We cannot disregard it; rather we must own up to it and learn from it.

And that is the intersection at which we stand right now. Instead of turning our backs on it totally we must probe it for a new definition of what mission is for this precise time on earth. The Matthew text is not that much of a has-been. New Testament scholars have put it in a new perspective for us during the last half century. It is probably not a direct quotation from Jesus, because the neat formula of the Trinity is used, a doctrine that was not solidified until much later in the history of the early church. It is not found in the other gospels, though a verse resembling it appears in Luke's writings: "But you shall receive power when the Holy Spirit has come upon you; and you shall be my witnesses in Jerusalem and in all Judea and Samaria and to the end of the earth." (Acts 1:8) The sacrament of baptism, quite obviously, had not become the entrance rite into an organized church during Jesus' own life. So today we have many reasons for not taking the Great Commission literally as a simple, easily defined command.

But its spirit remains and still bugs us—that is, we know that Jesus was passionate about certain things, and that his insistence upon getting things done that give birth to love, reconciliation and justice among men cannot be questioned. We can, therefore, breathe into Matthew's words what we feel to be the real impact of Christ's own priorities as we agonize over them in terms of today's world. And our discussion up to this point has been just that, an excursion through some dimensions of what we contemporary Christians call "mission."

If we take the word "baptizing," for example, and realize that before the complicated systems of sacraments and rituals of the church existed the word meant a symbolic act in which people expressed their desire for wholeness, health, freedom—even purity—we may come out closer to a first century understanding of the word. Immersion in water was that kind of symbol.

If we take the formula "in the name of" and set aside, for the moment, that strange concept of the "three-in-one God," and think rather of the loving Christ's human passion, God understood as "for others," we may come out with a keener idea of early Christian motives.

If we couple these two ideas, we may come out with a paraphrase like this: "driven by the force of Christ's own living for others, strive to immerse the world in the stream flowing toward wholeness, freedom, full human life, communicating to them through what you are and do just what he has become for you." In this sense, all peoples can become "disciples" of the Eternal—in their common devotion to freeing the billions of humans on the earth for maximum exercise of their potentialities, their mental and physical capacities, in the greatest possible concert with one another. Toward that end the secular Christian can work out his sense of mission, and toward that end the church can commit itself to being a catalytic agent. This marks the kind of "conversion" that we seek; a transforming of values and orientation toward the common possibilities of man.

It follows that the church continues to have a unique and pertinent role, because it must hound everybody, literally, with the great human imperatives and the eternal values that energize people to act like humans and not dumb animals. But it does not do so in the abstract, or in a vacuum or from a standpoint of superiority. As Christians we can endorse the United Nations' great "Universal Declaration of Human Rights," which states the major objective of our mission. And yet we are duty bound to be dissenters when members of the UN, including our own nation, behave in disregard of it. Our loyalty is not to nation: it is to Christ. Sometimes out of Christian loyalty we will resist our nation's policies; at other times, out of the same loyalty, we will support it. The same goes for all other involvements. The ultimate mission, the peculiarity of our identification with it, will call us into ever new roles of servant and prophet.

From what some Protestants may consider to be an uncongenial source, a powerful clarification of mission has come in Pope Paul VI's encyclical letter, *Populorum Progressio* ("On the Development of Peoples"). He begins by saying, "The development of peoples has the church's close attention, particularly the development of those peoples who are striving to escape from hunger, misery, endemic diseases and ignorance; of those who are looking for a wider share in the benefits of civilization and a more active improvement of their human qualities; of those who are aiming purposefully at their complete fulfillment. Following on the second Vatican Ecumenical Council, a renewed consciousness of the demands of the Gospel makes it her duty to put herself at the service of all, to help them grasp their serious problem in all its dimensions and to convince them that solidarity in action at this turning point in human history is a matter of urgency."

Quoting from the text of *Pacem in Terris,* the great encyclical by Pope John XXIII calling for world peace, Pope Paul makes these observations: "Local and individual undertakings are no longer enough. The present situation of the world demands concerted action based on a clear vision of all economic, social, cultural, and spiritual aspects. Experienced in human affairs, the church '. . . seeks but a solitary goal; to carry forward the work of Christ Himself under the lead of the befriending spirit. And Christ entered this world to give witness to the truth, to rescue and not sit in judgment, to serve and not to be served.' . . . Since the church lives in history, she ought to 'scrutinize the signs of the times and interpret them in the light of the Gospel.' Sharing the noblest aspirations of men and suffering when she sees them not satisfied, she wishes to help them attain their full flowering, and that is why she offers men what she possesses as her characteristic attribute: a global vision of man and of the human race."

Pope Paul lists specific targets. "Less human conditions: The lack of material necessities for those who are without the minimum essential for life, the moral deficiencies of those who are mutilated by selfishness. Less human conditions: Oppressive social structures, whether due to the abuses of ownership or to the abuses of power, to the exploitation of workers or to unjust transactions. Conditions that are more human: The passage from misery toward the possession of necessities, victory over social scourges, the growth of knowledge, the acquisition of culture. Additional conditions that are more human: Increased esteem for the dignity of others, the turning toward the spirit of poverty, cooperation for the common good, the will and desire for peace. Conditions that are still more human: The acknowledgment by man of supreme values, and of God their source and their finality. Conditions that, finally and above all, are more human: Faith, a gift of God accepted by the goodwill of man, and unity in the charity of Christ, who calls us all to share as sons in the life of the living God, the Father of all men." [1]

These words provide frameworks for our understanding "mission" in terms of humanizing the planet, becoming involved at every sector where we have talents and skills in order that some new breakout may occur in favor of persons. The break-up of the church's confidence in an abstract set of doctrines and an other-worldly faith has become a positive development, not a negative one. It means that we are forced to enter the fray of planetary existence with humility, or humiliation, and that our heritage has a chance of being understood as we identify ourselves with the struggles of the human race. Our uniqueness lies in Christ's reasons for getting involved, the ultimate hope in man's possibilities, a hope based upon past and present glimmerings of real breakthrough in the experiences of common people of the nature and characteristics of power.

The church's communication of a living word, a word of ultimate hope, of God's affirmation of life, lies in between the church's theological reflections about what it is called to do in the world, and what it actually ends up doing in the world. The world hears the actual message we send out loud and clear, and whether or not the world will respond to it depends on how well the church has done its homework, has come to terms with itself, has begun to comprehend the world and then does its theology. Generally speaking, the actual message the world hears is that we don't know what we're doing, that we've failed to come to terms with anything, that we've done no homework and that we can't get with the language of the real world. As Albert van den Heuvel, former director of the Youth Department of the World Council of Churches, has put it: "The church's mission today is to bring the scandal of the gospel within the hearing distance of secular man."

By the time this book gets into print the writer may well have changed occupations. At the moment I am a clergyman working within the organization of a giant denominational national staff, a bureaucrat, really. Renewal and *breakout* are needed on this level as much, if not more, than any other level of the church's missionary life. But I know a hotel executive who is performing incredible ministries from his desk, and the television network producer for whom I have written some scripts is bringing off little revolutions within the structure where he is housed. The former is a Roman Catholic; the latter, a Unitarian. The three of us are united in our understanding of mission. Lawyers, doctors, social workers, nurses, housewives and teachers share the same unity. I may take a different job within the church—a pastor of a congregation, perhaps— or I may go to an entirely different field of work. It all depends on how my continually growing understanding of myself and my capacities and my perceptions of the world change. But I do have a strong feeling about the church's mission and will always understand myself as standing under the call of Christ's imperatives.

Stuck in my mind are the words of one of the Fugs over National Educational Television recently: "I want the day to come when everybody lives in one giant polyethylene bag full of Vaseline." That would be beautiful; real flower power would at least be unleashed. (Jesus advocated flower power; remember what he said about the "birds of the air" and the "lilies of the field.") The affluent Christian today is caught in all sorts of tensions, and his situation is quite likely to remain this way. He loves the glory and grace of life itself, the grand colors and motions of the abundant life, but he is haunted by the fact that millions of humans crawl under rocks, powerless to change their own lot. He enjoys himself, but he restricts himself. He explores every kind of freedom possible, but he is burdened by the responsibility of a universal family. He dreams soaring thoughts and performs magnificent deeds; but he halts at the walls of his limited bags.

In short, he is bonded, through his specific baptism, to a movement that disciplines him. His view of life is hilarious and somber, both at once. It's a tightrope, gloriously miserable and miserably glorious. It's a paradox. A psychiatrist stated in a seminar on communication recently: "In the past fifty years man has learned decisive new things about everything in the universe—except who man is."

None of this is new. Ancient Hebrews sweated out the same dilemma. God? Where is he? Here? There? What? The language of the Psalms. A creative mystery lurks through it all and emerges through the spectacle of humans growing up, maturing and building each other up in love. That's very good news.

Upon these oddball, inconsistent handles more and more of us are hanging with the church today. They are our own summations of a very old spiritual insight:

The Spirit of the Lord is upon me,
because he has anointed me to preach good news to the
  poor.
He has sent me to proclaim release to the captives
and recovering of sight to the blind,
to set at liberty those who are oppressed,
to proclaim the acceptable year of the Lord.

Isaiah 61:1-2

Jesus read these words in the synagogue once, and the people threw him out of town for being so arrogant as to think that the words referred to him. But they did, and they refer to us, his brothers. That is our arrogance today, and we live with it gladly and nervously, in boldness and in humiliation. The Youngbloods sing about it, too:

Lollipops and revelation
Up and tumble time commotion
Blinking lights and blowing minds and glad with every-
  thing in motion
Reach out grab the stars
Try to find the way
Make yourself a place in the up and coming day. . . .
A nightmare to the ones who came before
Peeking through a hole in the futuristic door
And the merry-go-round goes around
The old yellow leaves keep fallin' to the ground
The world has been turned upside down behind making a
  new sound.[2]

Notes

Chapter 1

1. Copyright © 1966. Wingate Music Corporation, 1330 Avenue of Americas, New York, N.Y. All Rights Reserved. Used by permission.
2. "Psalm" by Richard Brautigan. *The San Francisco Review,* Vol. I, No. 2 (Spring, 1959).

Chapter 2

1. Reprinted by permission of Flute Publications. Copyright by Jane Stembridge. First published in *I Play Flute* (Tougaloo, Mississippi) 1967.

Chapter 3

1. Copyright © 1953 by Stanley Kunitz. By permission of Atlantic-Little, Brown and Company.

Chapter 4

1. *Reprinted from Christianity and Crisis,* Feb. 20, 1967; copyright 1967 by Christianity and Crisis, Inc.

Chapter 5

1. *Christians in the Technological and Social Revolutions of Our Time* by J. Brooke Mosley. By permission of Forward Movement Publications.
2. *Op. cit.*

Chapter 6

1. Anonymous. By permission of the editors of *Essence* (Vol. VIII, No. 1).
2. "Man, That's Real Swingin' Love" by David F. Marshall. *United Church Herald,* April, 1967.

Chapter 7

1. "Listen: Youth Speaks!" Copyright April, 1967 *Presbyterian Survey.* Reprinted with permission.
2. "I Built A Church" by Diane E. Mann. By permission of the editors of *Essence* (Vol. VIII, No. 1).

Chapter 8

1. *"The Coming Era of Ecumenopolis"* by Constantinos Doxiadis. *The Saturday Review* March 18, 1967. Reprinted by permission.
2. From *Lip Service,* by Martin Glass. Reprinted by permission of Students for a Democratic Society.

Chapter 9

1. Reprinted with permission of the Council of Churches of Christ of Greater Cleveland.
2. Dylan Thomas, *Collected Poems*. Copyright 1953 by Dylan Thomas. Reprinted by permission of New Directions Publishing Corporation.

Chapter 10

1. Reprinted courtesy of United States Catholic Conference.
2. "Merry-Go-Round" by Felix Pappalardi and Gail Collins. Copyright © 1967 Windfall Music Ent., Inc., 185 East 85th St., New York, N.Y. 10028. Performed by "The Youngbloods."

Guides and How to Live With Them

"This is Zok. See him run. Run, Zok, run!"

by Henry R. Martin (*Saturday Review*. Reprinted by permission.)

This is it. Now it comes!

You knew that there had to be a catch somewhere and here it is—the guide. We've talked about all these swinging and way out forms of mission and now I want to talk about a guide

—Ugh! "You call us to action and now you want us to sit down and talk!"

You feel betrayed? Well, hang on a little longer.

The last thing anyone wants to do is stifle the excitement that you feel about possibilities for Christian mission. Still, a note of warning must be sounded. Those cats—even the young ones—who go around turning the world upside down do it because they know what they want to do and are prepared to do it. This doesn't mean to say that they have some master blueprint in front of them and that they won't move without clear directions. On the contrary, they are people of action, but their action is grounded in their commitment. This is where the guide comes in. The guide should give you some help in plotting your direction and your action. Something like, for example, what Jesus and the disciples did when they cut out from the crowds and spent some time learning and discussing together.

So don't be afraid of the guide—for even though it involves some hard work it will add meaning and direction to your life of action.

A Clue or Two

Now a few clues about using this guide. First, if you don't like it don't get hung up on it. It's a guide and nothing else—it isn't meant to be a textbook. Our hope is that the cartoons, comments and questions may be of help to you. So let yourself go!

The guidance is designed to help you to enter into dialogue with some of the ideas and to further explore some of the subjects the book raises. You don't have to rely just on my words, and this is why we have given you additional sources that should aid you in your discussion and plans.

Cartoons

The cartoons are meant to be "starters," and they should be used as such. If they don't say anything to you, you shouldn't feel like you have to give some kind of answer. However, the cartoons were chosen for a purpose, and that fact should be a guide to take them seriously, at least.

Biblical Passages

You should not avoid the biblical passages that are suggested. The Bible still remains the source and guide for our Christian living. What we are after is not some literal or limited approach but the Christian "style." The Bible may not always set forth the specific solutions that we would like to have, but its style, or essence, still makes sense for us today. Don't forget to use a reliable biblical dictionary and commentary.

Well, now, the guide is yours, Swing into it and with it, for —who knows—we may be on the verge of a *breakout.*

Bags or
Search and Destroy Our Precious Cocoons

THE SMALL SOCIETY—By Brickman

by Morrie Brickman (*The Washington Star.* Reprinted by permission.)

Before we go any further, let's go around the group and see what this cartoon says to each of you. I'm going to throw in

133

part of what it says to me, but don't worry—I won't spoil things all the time!

Look at the signs and you see that they have all got the word "out" in them. The signs point to certain groups who want out of the bags that are suffocating them—and they want out quickly! These kinds of "outs" may seem irresponsible to some of you, but when the bags begin to suffocate, then people want out any way they can.

To See and Isolate Our Bags

Breaking out of bags isn't easy, whether they be your own, the church's or society's. To see and isolate the bags is hard enough, but to pierce through them is even harder. You are lucky that you have the chance to start this process in the comparative safety of your group. But it takes honesty and openness to be involved in this search; for often people refuse to admit that prejudice, smallness of vision, and other bags surround them.

QUESTION 1.

What prevents people from identifying the bags that surround them and limit them? ("People" includes you!)

To Open Up Our Bags

I can't think of any better source for looking at this question than the life of Jesus. Much of his ministry was devoted to individual encounters through which he helped people to see, and if they wanted to, to get out of their bags. Look at a few of the incidents that are listed below:

John 4:7-30; 39-42
Luke 19:1-10
John 21:15-19
Luke 6:1-11

Much of contemporary literature and art is aimed at exposing society's bags. Can you think of any book, play or film that seeks to do this?

QUESTION 2

Why does Jesus spend much of his ministry breaking bags? What does this say about the mission of the church?

Whose Bags Are Our Bags?

The question may be asked what is the Christian's responsibility beyond his own bags? It raises all sorts of questions about bags that surround and limit our communities, nation and world.

You should keep this question before you as you go through the guide, because this is what the book and the guide are all about.

QUESTION 3

Name some of the bags that you can identify that surround your own understanding of what the realities of the world are.

Sources

Hall, Kenneth F. and D. P. McGeachy, III, *How I Became the World's Strongest 96½ Pound Weakling.* (New York: Friendship) 1968.

Urban-Suburban or
We Live in Two Different Worlds

by Morrie Turner (Reproduced from the *Philadelphia Bulletin* by permission of The Register and Tribune Syndicate.)

Do you memember all the buttons that came out after the first clamor over black power? There was "green power," "youth power," "Irish power," "Italian power" and even "flower power." These were taken as a joke—either because they were already reality or they had no hope of becoming real. But when we mention "black power" everyone seems to get hung up. (We'll come back to this question in a later chapter.) This reaction shows the kind of problems that exist when we talk about urban and suburban living. A wall has arisen that makes these names seem like two different worlds that have no real relationship to each other.

QUESTION 1

This is an area where nearly all of us can act; very few of us do not live in one of these worlds. We could add that this is a problem where we *have* to act. Here is an opportunity for any group—either urban or suburban—to give a lead and guidance to many well-meaning, stumbling adults. And if you are prepared to act, don't take HUB or US and try and force it into your situation. Learn from others but try to work out a pattern and a strategy that suits your world—your city and suburbs.

QUESTION 2

In your community what efforts are being made similar to the US and HUB groups? If there are none, how do you account for this?

We Need Each Other

The really tragic aspect of the urban-suburban split is that people fail to recognize that they have much to contribute to each other—in fact, they need each other. Wherever the gaps have been bridged there has come the discovery that each area has its problems and its contributions to make. Instead of believing that we live in two different worlds, there is the realization that it is one world even as it relates to the city-suburb separation. It is still too easy to feel that they are two different worlds; hence anything that can help break down the barriers is of value.

Even the opportunity simply to hear what "the other side" has to say is important. Surely any group could arrange this kind of meeting.

QUESTION 3.

How could your group become involved in seeking better and closer relationships with persons "on the other side" of the urban-suburban split? (You should examine what are some of the difficulties that prevent you from involvement with people of other races and areas.)

Sources

Luke 10:29-37

Smith, Eugene L., *Mandate for Mission* (New York: Friendship) 1968.

The Arts or
Voices That Won't Be Quiet

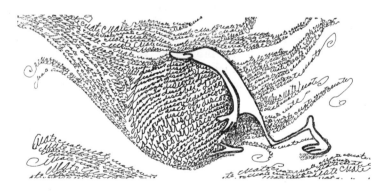

There is so much that a group of Christian youth can do in this area that it's hard to know where to begin. Apart from the dialogue or encounter with the artist himself, there is the whole variety of the arts that are now available to us all. Here is a way that we can have our eyes opened and our vision extended and our self-understanding enlarged. The contribution of the arts to the whole process of being human is being rediscovered with an exciting vengeance!

Here is a situation in which stereotypes are particularly dangerous, for if we aren't careful we can miss what the artist is trying to say. To say "I like it" or "I don't like it" after a cursory examination really misses the point. Don't get me wrong—artists and their work are not above criticism—in fact they are an invitation to criticism and discussion but we have to "hear" them, honestly and openly, if we want to benefit from their contribution. This is an area where there is no "right" or "wrong," but only contribution.

QUESTION 1

How would you describe your image of a "typical" artist?

Exciting and creative programs can be built around the arts. *Discover and Create* (see Sources) is a packet designed to help you discover and create within the arts. The arts have a way of opening both us and our world! Don't be afraid to take them on.

But the kind of challenge that the arts bring is not confined to painting, sculpture or Broadway. Take, for example, the movies or television. Much of their material may be second class, but there is also much of value and significance.

QUESTION 2

Recall a recent play, movie or television program that you liked; how would you relate it to a dialogue between the church and the arts?

Now let's go back to the arts packet labelled *Discover and Create*. Before we answer question 3, let's try our own hand at the arts, being critical of the "happening" described in Chapter 3. You may be able to develop your own happening.

QUESTION 3

What do you think of the happening that the author describes as a significant experience?

Sources

Abels, Paul and Barbara, *Discover and Create* (New York: Friendship) 1968.

motive magazine, p.o. box 871, Nashville, Tenn.

Sister Corita, *Footnotes and Headlines: A play-pray book* (New York: Herder and Herder) 1967.

Dunbar, Paul Laurence, *The Complete Poems of Paul Laurence Dunbar.* (New York: Dodd, Mead) 1962.

Hughes, Langston, *The Best of Simple* (New York: Holt, Rhinehart and Winston) 1953.

Protest or
To Protest or Not to Protest

Is That the Question?

"Every man has his price, they say."

Drawing by Opie; © 1967 The New Yorker Magazine, Inc.

This is the program where we will touch a few raw nerves. The only way you can avoid these "gut" issues is to avoid the chapter—but that would be stupid. As long as we are divided over major issues, nothing can be solved by avoiding them. In fact, it has been the avoidance of many of these questions that has led to the serious situation that now confronts us. One of the reasons why some of the acts of protest become desperate is that groups are not talking to each other. Whatever happens, don't be talked out of doing something because the issues are "too controversial." These are the issues that confront us all *now* and they demand our attention.

Facts Before Fiction

There is a real danger that we could discuss some of these issues and all we would be doing is pooling our ignorance. Take a controversial issue or two and set your group the task of finding out all the *facts* they can about it. Have a look at historical precedents and the biblical witness as well as contemporary sources and be diligent in your search. One of the ways we learn the truth is to seek after it!

Programs on Protest

You could build programs around each of the questions listed below without any difficulty, and they would probably prove to be exciting ones. One of the most controversial questions is the involvement of the church in many of the great questions and problems of our time.

For each of the questions, I want to suggest a bit of homework and see how you answer the question after doing some checking out.

The Church and the Nazis

See how much you can find out about the witness of the church during the Nazi regime in Germany. It is a fascinating story, but make sure you look at it from all sides and include both those who supported and those who opposed Hitler. Keep your results in mind as you try and answer question 1. This is an extreme example, but what might have happened if the voices of protest had been raised earlier?

QUESTION 1

What do you feel about Christians being involved in protest movements?

Kodak and FIGHT

Reference is made in chapter 4 to the struggle between Kodak and FIGHT in Rochester. Here was the church, acting as an institution, trying to pressure Kodak into making certain changes. This story still goes on, and the results have justified the action of the church—but is this always the case? What do you think about the church using its power in this way?

QUESTION 2

What about churches as institutions getting mixed up in politics? Black Power?

Why not have a program in which you get a black power advocate to come and speak to your group? There is a great deal of misunderstanding of what the term means, and even to its various proponents it means different things. It would pay the group to have a look at some of the various views of black power that have been put forward and try and work out some of the different approaches that black power advocates have.

QUESTION 3

How do you and people in your home, school and church feel about black power?

Violence

The violence of recent summers has brought this question close to all of us. There is little indication that the problem will go away. Before we glibly answer question 4 it would pay us to have a look at violence in the history of North America.

H. Rap Brown says, "It's as American as blueberry pie." And we have to go behind the headlines and emotional statements and ask ourselves a lot of questions. What drives a man to violence? Is anything achieved by violence? What would you do in a totally desperate situation? Now try to answer question 4.

QUESTION 4

Can a Christian ever participate in activities that lead to violence? Justify your answer in terms of ghetto revolts and political revolutions in places like Latin America, Asia and Africa.

Sources

Brandt, Joseph R., *Why Black Power?* (New York: Friendship) 1968.

Debray, Regis, *Revolution in the Revolution?* (New York: Grove) 1967.

DuBois, W. E. B., *The Souls of Black Folk* (Greenwich, Conn.: Fawcett) 1953.

Ellison, Ralph, *The Invisible Man* (New York: Random House) 1947.

Peace or
Will We Make It?

Reprinted by permission of Johnny Hart and Publishers—Hall Syndicate.

Is there any question that dominates our headlines as much as the question of peace and war? Things may have changed during the interval between the writing of this guide and now, when you use it, but peace will not likely have come to our troubled world. There is hardly a section of our globe that does not have some kind of war or strife between peoples and nations. And sadly, there seems the promise of much more to come. Peace is tied in with many problems, and often a war is only the symbol of the underlying frustrations and problems. But it has become a life and death matter for us all because we are all aware of the tremendous destructive forces that man has at his disposal. *Dr. Strangelove, Fail-Safe, The War Game* and *On The Beach* are a few of the films that have tried to depict the dangers and the horrors of nuclear power.

This is still another situation in which a drastic reappraisal may be necessary for us to come close to the truth. And the stakes are very high.

East Versus West?

Let's take, for example the supposed struggle between communism and the West. Here we find very significant changes over the last few years. We have watched the growing struggle between two great communist powers; we have traded increasingly with Eastern European countries; Canada has carried out considerable trade with China. Add to this the growing exchanges between Russia and North America on the cultural level and we see a genuine softening of the cold war. Now try question 1.

QUESTION 1

How do you feel about the author's contention that communists and Christians ought to be in dialogue with each other, perhaps even cooperate?

Against War or For Peace?

Historically, people have often spoken of "the just war." Do you support such a theory? You may. Write down a list of reasons for and against war. You will probably come up with a list that will have a lot of "ifs" and "buts" and this is to be expected. Some of you may feel strongly that war is never justified while others may believe that it is a way of solving some of the problems of our time. After you have done this, why not do the same for peace and see what you come up with. (See that you remember your discussion on violence and check whether it has any relationship to the question of war and peace.)

QUESTION 2

What are your views, as a Christian, about the conflict in Vietnam? The Middle East? Africa—the Congo, Nigeria?

It's Your Responsibility

It is an easy out to place such a problem as this into the laps of the politicians and say that we can't do anything about it. You can do something and should. Apart from the fact that many of you will be reaching voting age fairly soon, you do have a role in creating a climate in which peace discussions can be carried on. You could also be a force in helping to determine the kind of public witness that your church will make. So don't chicken out—it's too big a subject for that.

QUESTION 3

Reflect on Mr. Ige's speech in terms of your own nationality.

QUESTION 4

What are the implications of that speech for you as a future voter?

Sources

Isaiah 60:1-5
Isaiah 61:1-11
Matt. 5:38-48
Rutenber, Culbert G., *Peace Keeping or Peace Making?* (New York: Friendship Press) 1968.

Get material from your denominational board that is working in this area. (This applies for all subjects—a chance to find out about the broader work of your church.)

Personhood or
Human Beings Who Aren't Human (For Me)

"Arise, Sir or Madame..."

by Ed Fisher (*Saturday Review.* Reprinted by permission.)

The dangerous thing about this subject is that it is very easy to violate the personhood of others without realizing what we have done. The cartoon above speaks to a fairly common feeling about long hair—yet there have been many times in history when long hair stood for manliness and strength. Anyone who has grown a beard will tell you stories about how people's attitudes towards him changed after he grew it. And so you could go on—try clothes, beards, long hair—and sometimes just being a young person—and you will find people who will deny you your rights as a person. And there are more serious examples, like the story of a reporter in *Black Like Me*.

QUESTION 1

What are the predominant stereotypes in your community about persons who are considered in some way to be socially unacceptable?

Misfits

Some of the examples given above may be on the borderline but there are a number of groups in society that lose their personhood *in toto* because of who or what they are.

You could draw up a list of these, and I am sure that it would include some of the following: homosexuals, prostitutes, ex-convicts, and so on. But don't think that it is easy to grant them their personhood. Some of us rarely come in contact with this kind of person, and even if we do there is a thin line between acceptance of the person and tacit approval of what he may stand for.

QUESTION 2

With whom do you have the greatest conflict about your associations with questionable people, moral "misfits," etc.?

The Law and Personhood

One of the most difficult aspects of our examination of this subject comes when we realize that even the law itself may deny people their personhood. Can you think of any examples of laws that treat some persons unjustly? To oppose these can often bring contempt and ridicule from our peers. In the question below we have raised a number of subjects that are under review in the United States, Canada and other nations. Take the various parts of the question one at a time and see how you come out.

QUESTION 3

Describe your attitudes about changes in laws about homosexuality, abortion, the death penalty, drinking and voting age.

A Ministry

Here is a kind of ministry that the church should and must fulfill. If we take the example of Jesus then we find a constant concern for people whom society would not accept. Sometimes it was a leper, other times a prostitute and sometimes a religious outcast. Jesus showed no hesitancy or embarrassment at doing this. In fact, in doing this he showed his own humanity.

We mentioned in chapter 6 some of the night ministries that are being performed in various parts of North America. (Why should night so often be associated with sin?) Not all of us can carry on this kind of ministry, but *all* of us can do our share in seeing that people around us are not denied their personhood through prejudice, misunderstanding and middle-class morals.

QUESTION 4

What do you think about the illustrations of lay people and clergy being involved with "night people" and others?

Sources

John 7:53–8:11
Naylor, Phyllis Reynolds, *When Rivers Meet* (New York: Friendship) 1968.

Congregations or
Too Late! Too Late?

"Harry was always rather conservative."

by William P. Hoest (*Saturday Review*. Reprinted by permission.)

It is very easy to criticize your local congregation. Yet we should have some awareness of what we are dealing with—an institution 1900 years old. It is the longest running institution in the West! This may help us to understand, but it does not make us any more sympathetic to the "horse and buggy" church in the jet age.

Similarly, we must realize that we are dealing with an organization that means a great deal to many people. Some are more than hesitant to allow any change, in fact they would

148

like to turn the clock back! This is not true of all members of the church but it is for many—so don't be surprised when you encounter them and try to understand.

What's Your Congregation Like?

Let's examine the three congregations that have been described in chapter 7 and see which one fits (or is at least close) to your church. Do *all* congregations fit these broad descriptions?

QUESTION 1

How is the author fair or unfair in his descriptions of the three congregations? Are they similar to your views?

What Is Mission for the Local Congregation?

Much discussion has taken place in recent years about the mission of the local church. A good deal of this study has come from the World Council of Churches in its famous *Life and Mission* studies. Names like Colin Williams, Bill Webber, Stephen Rose spring to mind as leaders in the thinking about the mission of the local church.

The question below relates to *your* congregation. Before you answer it, why not do a poll of your leaders and see what definitions they come up with. Appoint a member or two of your group to be a "roving reporter" and get the leaders' responses taped in time for your meeting.

QUESTION 2

What examples can you find in your own church of the popular images of "mission" given?

Take an outspoken student's comments and see what you can make of them.

QUESTION 3

Do you agree or disagree with the outspoken student's demands? Why?

Now that you've read the chapter and questions, what kinds of mission do you think are needed in your congregation?

Sources

Jeremiah 18:1-12

Rev. 3:14-22

Cavanaugh, James, *A Modern Priest Looks at His Outdated Church* (New York: Trident) 1967.

Cox, Harvey, *God's Revolution and Man's Responsibility* (New York: Judson Press) 1965.

Davenport, Gene L., *What's the Church For?* (New York: Friendship) 1968.

Waters, Richard D., *Dangerfield Newby Moves Uptown* (New York: Friendship) 1968.

Williams, Colin, *What in the World?* (New York: Council Press) 1965.

Williams, Colin, *Where in the World?* (New York: Council Press) 1963.

Look Back and Dream. Recording. (New York: Friendship Press) 1968.

The New Scene or
A New Day and a New World

Reprinted by permission of Johnny Hart and Publishers—Hall Syndicate.

In looking at the new scene we should look at both the church and the world. There is a new scene in the church but there is also a new world. The new scene Christian will have to know his world or his mission won't minister to the world in which he lives.

The New World

You are part of this new world, but don't take it for granted. The new world is full of promise, but a great peril continually haunts its stage. As our technology moves forward at an ever increasing pace we're told we're losing the battle against hunger and poverty in many parts of the world. The staggering fact is that the rich are getting richer and the poor poorer! As long as this situation exists the new world will never fulfill its promise.

The New Church

In the last chapter we discussed some of the problems of local congregations. Now look at the new scene as it exists in the church at large. If you didn't get the message before, let me make sure you get it now: I'm excited about the new scene that's emerging in the church! but it's a road fraught with danger and costly responsibiilty, but one we can't avoid.

QUESTION 1

The author lists three primary questions involved in mission. Summarize what your understanding of them is, and give some illustrations from your experience of persons or groups who seem to be facing them.

Let's take our questions in this study very seriously. Appoint a reporter and keep track of what you say or decide. See what concrete illustrations you can come up with. It's easy to criticize, but see what you can discover in a creative way.

The next question is about a subject that has made many religious headlines: the unity of the churches. Before you answer the question, make a list of ecumenical activity in your own area. See how it fits in with your answer to the question that follows.

QUESTION 2

What do you think about the new burst of ecumenical activity among churches? What seem to be the greatest problems in the effort toward church unity?

Questions 3 and 4 belong together, so let's do them that way. Go carefully through Dr. Glatthorn's argument, and see where you stand.

QUESTION 3

Where do you stand in relation to Dr. Glatthorn's action?

QUESTION 4

How do you feel about the ambiguity which the author insists is inevitable in the church's work?

Sources

2 Cor. 5:16-21

Rev. 21:1-8

Boulding, Kenneth, *The Meaning of the 20th Century: The Great Transition* (New York: Harper) 1964.

Cox, Harvey, *The Secular City* (New York: Macmillan) 1965.

Daedalus "The Year 2000" Vol. 96, No. 3 (Summer, 1967).

Hall, Cameron P. ed., *Human Values and Advancing Technology* (New York: Friendship) 1967.

Renewal and Breakout or Christianity a Go-Go?

Reprinted by permission of Johnny Hart and Publishers—Hall Syndicate.

Don't you love that cartoon? True of the church? Perhaps, but we have been leading up to the fact that something is happening and something could happen! It's up to you. We're passing you the ball.

So let's start by an examination of the church as you know it, and the attempts at renewal and breakout. Then let's examine the reactions we have to the radical things that the author describes. Don't stop here. The emphasis now is for ACTION! We can't renew or breakout unless we act.

Renewal

Renewal means taking something that is old and "renewing" it. For the church, renewal means that there are things worth saving and rebuilding. What do you think is worth renewing in your church? Or is everything okay?

QUESTION 1

How would you characterize the institutional church as you know it in your own life?

Breakout

Breakout really suggests a new pattern, including new structures and organizations. For example, would you say that the Protestant Reformation was a renewing of the church, a breakout or both? Remember Luther and Calvin did build on the old but what emerged was a new set of structures. Try and get an "expert" (your minister, a college or high school history instructor, to tell you something more about the complexities of the Reformation).

When you discuss question 2, make sure you differentiate between renewal efforts and breakout efforts. You might also ask why it's necessary to sometimes breakout rather than renew more slowly.

QUESTION 2

List some examples from your area of renewal and breakout efforts.

153

Jesus Mission: Renewal and Breakout

The life and mission of Jesus provides a fascinating example of what we have been talking about. It would be easy to argue that Jesus was a renewer ("Think not that I have come to destroy the law but to fulfill the law.") But a strong case could also be made that Jesus was really a breakout expert.

Let's ask a few questions about Jesus and his mission and see if it helps us with our renewal-breakout problem. Do you think Jesus was essentially an innovator, i.e. working from the old to apply it to his own scene, or a radical in the sense that he initiated new things? Why did the "established church" of his time oppose him so vigorously? Would this or does this happen today when radicals try to breakout?

QUESTION 3

Where are you likely to find opposition in your attempts at renewal and breakout? Will the reasons for opposition be mainly theological, pragmatic or personal?

Sources

Renewal magazine, Chicago, Ill.
Ramparts magazine, San Francisco, Cal.

For more information about current programs of renewal and breakout, write the following for information:
The Ecumenical Institute, Chicago, Ill.
East Harlem Protestant Parish, New York, N.Y.
Church of the Savior, Washington, D.C.
Community Renewal Society, Chicago, Ill.
Experimental Ministries, DCLM, National Council of Churches, 475 Riverside Drive, New York, N.Y. 10027

Mission Impossible or Christians Aren't Chicken

"Can't you make her smile?"

Drawing by B. Petty; © 1967 The New Yorker Magazine, Inc.

Well, this is the last study, and the word is GO! The world becomes the stage, but we aren't actors. This is for real. The world is writing an agenda that's crowded with urgent items and the task is yours. The mission does look impossible. But what are the alternatives? We could put our heads in the sand and hope that the problems will go away, but this won't work. It's easy to say that it's not *my* responsibility and leave it to others, but anyone who claims or is claimed by the Christian gospel must accept responsibility as Christ has accepted him. So it looks like we're stuck with the problem. We just have to do the best we can.

155

You Are Not Alone

All through this book we've been trying to tell you that you're not on your own, and that there are many forces inside and outside the church that we're called on to cooperate with. One of the exciting discoveries of our time that the church has made (or remade) is that God *is* at work in the world, and that's where the action is. If you're really serious about this mission, you'll learn what movements and institutions apart from the church are helping to fulfill humanity. Jesus put it another way when he chastised the disciples for their limited vision, saying that he who is not against us is for us. It would be a good exercise to check what groups are at work in your community trying to achieve mission impossible. You might start by exploring some of the groups that we've mentioned in the book.

QUESTION 1

How do you feel about the author's interpretation of the Great Commission?

QUESTION 2

Do you think that Pope Paul's encyclical is realistic? Why?

The Mission and Yourself

So far we haven't put too much pressure on you directly, but before we conclude you should take a look at the contribution you intend to make through your vocation, church life and responsibilities in the community. It's corny but true: we all have a part to play in bringing the world to the fullness of its humanity. Another important by-product is that in attempting this we bring ourselves to life and humanity. "Whoever would lose his life . . . will save it."

Let's examine vocation for a moment or two. Not everyone can be a doctor, nurse, poverty worker or overseas agricultural expert, yet our vocations are of great importance to us and to the world for its humanizing process. The Christian must carefully examine his motives and hopes in deciding on his vocation.

QUESTION 3

What kinds of things have you considered doing as an occupation? Can you evaluate them in terms of the author's idea of mission as humanizing the planet?

Perhaps this last question is a strange way to end. Many of you may have felt that I have been arrogant, harsh, judgmental and so on, and these all may be true. Yet there is a strong commitment to Christ and his mission. I hope that makes sense to you—it does to me.

QUESTION 4

Does the author's devotion to the church make sense to you? Why?

Sources

Ezekiel 37:1-14
Joel 2:28-30
Gilkey, Langdon, *Shantung Compound* (New York: Harper) 1966.
Wolf, Wilmert, H. Jr., *Witness? I Couldn't—Could I?* (New York: Friendship) 1968.

For Your Follow-Up

Does what you have read in *Breakout* remind you of something? Perhaps you have faced problems and needs similar to those described in this book. If so, you may have found a new way of dealing with them, of ministering, of doing something constructive. In that case, your experiments, ideas and insights may be helpful to others.

The Department of Youth Ministry of the National Council of Churches is seeking to gather information about current experiments, whether "successful" or not. You can help, therefore, by sending:

—a letter, telling us what you think of *Breakout*.

—a description of some new thing you may have tried in youth ministry.

—a request for further information, as it becomes available, on specific kinds of youth ministry experiments in which you are vitally interested.

When you report a project in which you have been or are now involved, do more than describe it. Say what you think you and your group have learned from it and what, in your judgment, the project has accomplished.

Among the projects the Department is especially interested in hearing about are these:

—experimental ministries to youth in your community.

—new types of ecumenical encounter among young people.

—new ways of involving youth meaningfully in the total life of the church.

Your response should be addressed to
Data Bank
Department of Youth Ministry
National Council of Churches
475 Riverside Dr.—Room 832
New York, N. Y. 10027